Elements Essay Anthology

Edited by John Pfannkuchen.

Original essays by John Pfannkuchen and original authors, edited by John Pfannkuchen.

Elwood Learning

47 Vine St

Binghamton, NY 13903

www.elwoodlearning.com

Ordering Information:

Quantity sales. Special discounts are available on quantity purchases by corporations, associations, and others. For details, contact the publisher at the address above.

Orders by U.S. trade bookstores and wholesalers. Please contact Ingram Distribution at One Ingram Blvd., La Vergne, TN 37086 • 615.793.5000

For my students at the State University of New York Broome.

Elements

The Art of the Essayist

Arthur Benson

There is a pleasant story of an itinerant sign-painter who in going his rounds came to a village inn upon whose sign-board he had had his eye for some months and had watched with increasing hope and delight its rapid progress to blurred and faded dimness. To his horror he found a brand-new varnished sign. He surveyed it with disgust, and said to the inn-keeper, who stood nervously by hoping for a professional compliment, "This looks as if someone had been doing it himself."

That sentence holds within it the key to the whole mystery of essay-writing. An essay is a thing which someone does himself; and the point of the essay is not the subject, for any subject will suffice, but the charm of personality. It must concern itself with something "jolly," as the school-boy says, something smelt, heard, seen, perceived, invented, thought; but the essential thing is that the writer shall have formed his own impression, and that it shall have taken shape in his own mind; and the charm of the essay depends upon the charm of the mind that has conceived and recorded the impression. It will be seen, then, that the essay need not concern itself with anything definite; it need not have an intellectual or a philosophical or a religious or a humorous motif; but equally none of these subjects are ruled out. The only thing necessary is that the thing or the thought should be vividly apprehended, enjoyed, felt to be beautiful, and expressed with a certain gusto. It need conform to no particular rules. All literature answers to something in life, some habitual form of human expression. The stage imitates life, calling in the services of the eye and the ear; there is the narrative of the teller of tales or the minstrel; the song, the letter, the talk—all forms of human expression and communication have their antitypes in literature. The essay is the reverie, the frame of mind in which a man says, in the words of the old song, "Says I to myself, says I."

It is generally supposed that Montaigne is the first writer who wrote what may technically be called essays. His pieces are partly autobiographical, partly speculative, and to a great extent ethical. But the roots of his writing lie far back in literary history. He owed a great part of his inspiration to Cicero, who treated of abstract topics in a conversational way with a romantic background; and this he owed to Plato, whose dialogues undoubtedly contain the germ of both the novel and the essay. Plato is in truth far more the forerunner of the novelist than of the philosopher. He made a background of life, he peopled his scenes with bright boys and amiable elders—oh that all scenes were so peopled!—and he discussed ethical and speculative problems of life and character with a vital rather than with a philosophical interest. Plato's dialogues would be essays but for the fact that they have a dramatic coloring, while the essence of the essay is soliloquy. But in the writings of Cicero, such as the De Senectute, the dramatic interest is but slight, and the whole thing approaches far more nearly to the essay than to the novel. Probably Cicero supplied to his readers the function both of the essayist and the preacher, and fed the needs of so-called thoughtful readers by dallying, in a fashion which it is hardly unjust to call twaddling, with familiar ethical problems of conduct and character. The charm of Montaigne is the charm of personality—frankness, gusto, acute observation, lively acquaintance with men and manners. He is ashamed of recording nothing that interested him; and a certain discreet shamelessness must always be the characteristic of the essayist, for the essence of his art is to say what has pleased him without too prudently considering whether it is worthy of the attention of the well-informed mind.

I doubt if the English temperament is wholly favorable to the development of the essayist. In the first place, an Anglo-Saxon likes doing things better than thinking about them; and in his memories, he is apt to recall how a thing was done rather than why it was done. In the next place, we are naturally rather prudent and secretive; we say that a man must not wear his heart upon his sleeve, and that is just what the essayist must do. We have a horror of giving ourselves away, and we like to keep ourselves to ourselves. "The Englishman's home is his castle," says another proverb. But the essayist must not have a castle, or if he does, both the grounds and the living-rooms must be open to the inspection of the public.

Lord Brougham, who reveled in advertisement, used to allow his house to be seen by visitors, and the butler had orders that if a party of people came to see the house, Lord Brougham was to be informed of the fact. He used to hurry to the library and take up a book, in order that the tourists might nudge each other and say in whispers, "There is the Lord Chancellor." That is the right frame of mind for the essayist. He may enjoy privacy, but he is no less delighted that people should see him enjoying it.

The essay has taken very various forms in England. Sir Thomas Browne, in such books as Religio Medici and Urn-Burial, wrote essays of an elaborate rhetorical style, the long fine sentences winding themselves out in delicate weft-like trails of smoke on a still air, hanging in translucent veils. Addison, in the Spectator, treated with delicate humor of life and its problems, and created what was practically a new form in the essay of emotional sentiment evoked by solemn scenes and fine associations. Charles Lamb treated romantically the homeliest stuff of life, and showed how the simplest and commonest experiences were rich in emotion and humor. The beauty and dignity of common life were his theme. De Quincey wrote what may be called impassioned autobiography, and brought to his task a magical control of long-drawn and musical cadences. And then we come to such a writer as Pater, who used the essay for the expression of exquisite artistic sensation. These are only a few instances of the way in which the essay has been used in English literature. But the essence is throughout the same; it is personal sensation, personal impression, evoked by something strange or beautiful or curious or interesting or amusing. It has thus a good deal in common with the art of the lyrical poet and the writer of sonnets, but it has all the freedom of prose, its more extended range, its use of less strictly poetical effects, such as humor in particular. Humor is alien to poetical effect, because poetry demands a certain sacredness and solemnity of mood. The poet is emotional in a reverential way; he is thrilled, he loves, he worships, he sorrows; but it is all essentially grave, because he wishes to recognize the sublime and up-lifted elements of life; he wishes to free himself from all discordant, absurd, fantastic, undignified contrasts, as he would extrude laughter and chatter and comfortable ease from some stately act of ceremonial worship. It is quite true that the essayist has a full right to such a mood if he chooses; and such essays as Pater's are all conceived in a sort of rapture of holiness, in a region from which all that is common and homely is carefully fenced out. But the essayist may have a larger range, and the strength of a writer like Charles Lamb is that he condescends to use the very commonest materials, and transfigures the simplest experiences with a fairy-like delicacy and a romantic glow. A poet who has more in common with the range of the essayist Robert Browning, and there are many of his poems, though not perhaps his best, where his frank amassing of grotesque detail, his desire to include rather than exclude the homelier sorts of emotion, of robust and not very humorous humor, make him an impressionist rather than a lyrist. As literature develops, the distinction between poetry and prose will no doubt become harder to maintain. Coleridge said in a very fruitful maxim: "The opposite of poetry is not prose but science; the opposite of prose is not poetry but verse." That is to say poetry has as its object the kindling of emotion and science is its opposite, because science is the dispassionate statement of fact; but prose can equally be used as a vehicle for the kindling of emotion, and therefore may be in its essence poetical: but when it is a technical description of a certain kind of structure its opposite is verse—that is to say, language arranged in metrical and rhythmical form. We shall probably come to think that the essayist is more of a poet than the writer of epics, and that the divisions of literature will tend to be on the one hand the art of clear and logical statement, and on the other the art of emotional and imaginative expression.

We must remember in all this that the nomenclature of literature, the attempt to classify the forms of literary expression, is a confusing and a bewildering thing unless it is used merely for convenience. It is the merest pedantry to say that literature must conform to established usages and types. The essence of it is that it is a large force flowing in any channel that it can, and the classification of art is a mere classification of channels. What lies behind all art is the principle of wonder and of arrested attention. It need not be only the sense of beauty; it may be the sense of fitness, of strangeness, of completeness, of effective effort. The amazement of the savage at the sight of a civilized town is not the sense of beauty, it is the sense of force, of mysterious resources, of incredible pro-ducts, of things unintelligibly and even magically made; and then too there is the instinct for perceiving all that is grotesque, absurd, amusing and jocose, which one sees exhibited in children at the sight of the parrot's crafty and solemn eye and his exaggerated imitation of human speech, at the unusual dress and demeanor of the clown, at the grotesque simulation by the gnarled and contorted tree of something human or reptile. And then, too, there is the strange property in human beings which makes disaster amusing, if its effects are not prejudicial to oneself; that sense which makes the waiter on the pantomime stage, who falls headlong with a tray of crockery, an object to provoke the loudest and most spontaneous mirth of which the ordinary human being is capable. The moralist who would be sympathetically shocked at the rueful abrasions of the waiter, or mournful over the waste of human skill and endeavor involved in the breakage, would be felt by all human beings to have something priggish in his composition and to be too good, as they say, to live.

It is with these rudimentary and inexplicable emotions that the essayist may concern himself, even though the poet be forbidden to do so; and the appeal of the essayist to the world at large will depend upon the extent to which he experiences some common emotion, sees it in all its bearings, catches the salient features of the scene, and records it in vivid and impressive speech.

The essayist is therefore, to a certain extent, bound to be a spectator of life; he must be like the man in Browning's fine poem "How it Strikes a Contemporary," who walked about, took note of everything, looked at the new house building, poked his stick into the mortar.

> He stood and watched the cobbler at his trade,
>
> The man who slices lemons into drink,
>
> The coffee-roaster's brazier, and the boys
>
> That volunteer to help him turn its winch;
>
> He glanced o'er books on stalls with half an eye,
>
> And fly-leaf ballads on the vendor's string,
>
> And broad-edge bold-print posters by the wall;
>
> He took such cognizance of men and things!
>
> If any beat a horse, you felt he saw;
>
> If any cursed a woman, he took note,
>
> Yet stared at nobody—they stared at him,
>
> And found less to their pleasure than surprise,
>
> He seemed to know them, and expect as much.

That is the essayist's material; he may choose the scene, he may select the sort of life he is interested in, whether it is the street or the countryside or the sea-beach or the picture-gallery; but once there, wherever he may be, he must devote himself to seeing and realizing and getting it all by heart. The writer must not be too much interested in the action and conduct of life. If he is a politician, or a soldier, or an emperor, or a plough-boy, or a thief, and is absorbed in what he is doing, with a vital anxiety to make profit or position or influence out of it; if he hates his opponents and rewards his friends; if he condemns, despises, disapproves, he at once forfeits sympathy and largeness of view. He must believe with all his might in the interest of what he enjoys, to the extent at all events of believing it worth recording and representing, but he must not believe too solemnly or urgently in the importance and necessity of any one sort of business or occupation. The eminent banker, the social reformer, the forensic pleader, the fanatic, the crank, the puritan—these are not the stuff out of which the essayist is made; he may have ethical preferences, but he must not indulge in moral indignation; he must be essentially tolerant, and he must discern quality rather than solidity. He must be concerned with the pageant of life, as it weaves itself with a moving tapestry of scenes and figures rather than with the aims and purposes of life. He must, in fact, be preoccupied with things as they appear, rather than with their significance or their ethical example.

I have little doubt in my own mind that the charm of the familiar essayist depends upon his power of giving the sense of a good-humored, gracious and reasonable personality and establishing a sort of pleasant friendship with his reader. One does not go to an essayist with a desire for information, or with an expectation of finding a clear statement of a complicated subject; that is not the mood in which one takes up a volume of essays. What one rather expects to find is a companionable treatment of that vast mass of little problems and floating ideas which are aroused and evoked by our passage through the world, our daily employment, our leisure hours, our amusements and diversions, and above all by our relations with other people—all the unexpected, inconsistent, various simple stuff of life; the essayist ought to be able to impart a certain beauty and order into it, to delineate, let us say, the vague emotions aroused in solitude or in company by the sight of scenery, the aspect of towns, the impressions of art and books, the interplay of human qualities and characteristics, the half-formed hopes and desires and fears and joys that form so large a part of our daily thoughts. The essayist ought to be able to indicate a case or a problem that is apt to occur in ordinary life and suggest the theory of it, to guess what it is that makes our moods resolute or fitful, why we act consistently or inconsistently, what it is that repels or attracts us in our dealings with other people, what our private fancies are. The good essayist is the man who makes a reader say: "Well, I have often thought all those things, but I never discerned before any connection between them, nor got so far as to put them into words." And thus the essayist must have a great and far-reaching curiosity; he must be interested rather than displeased by the differences of human beings and by their varied theories. He must recognize the fact that most people's convictions are not the result of reason, but a mass of associations, traditions, things half-understood, phrases, examples, loyalties, whims. He must care more about the inconsistency of humanity than about its dignity; and he must study more what people actually do think about than what they ought to think about. He must not be ashamed of human weaknesses or shocked by them, and still less disgusted by them; but at the same time he must keep in mind the flashes of fine idealism, the passionate visions, the irresponsible humors, the salient peculiarities, that shoot like sun rays through the dull cloudiness of so many human minds, and make one realize that humanity is at once above itself and in itself, and that we are greater than we know; for the interest of the world to the ardent student of it is that we most of us seem to have got hold of something that is bigger than we quite know how to deal with; something remote and far off, which we have seen in a distant vision, which we cannot always remember or keep clear in our minds. The supreme fact of human nature is its duality, its tendency to pull different ways, the tug-of-war between Devil and Baker which lies inside our restless brains. And the confessed aim of the essayist is to make people interested in life and in themselves and in the part they can take in life; and he does that best if he convinces men and women that life is a fine sort of a game, in which they can take a hand; and that every existence, however confined or restricted, is full of outlets and pulsing channels, and that the interest and joy of it is not confined to the politician or the millionaire, but is pretty fairly distributed, so long as one has time to attend to it, and is not preoccupied in some concrete aim or vulgar ambition.

Because the great secret which the true essayist whispers in our ears is that the worth of experience is not measured by what is called success, but rather resides in a fullness of life: that success tends rather to obscure and to diminish experience, and that we may miss the point of life by being too important, and that the end of it all is the degree in which we give rather than receive.

The poet perhaps is the man who sees the greatness of life best, because he lives most in its beauty and fineness. But my point is that the essayist is really a lesser kind of poet, working in simpler and humbler materials, more in the glow of life perhaps than in the glory of it, and not finding anything common or unclean.

The essayist is the opposite of the romancer, because his one and continuous aim is to keep the homely materials in view; to face actual conditions, not to fly from them. We think meanly of life if we believe that it has no sublime moments; but we think sentimentally of it if we believe that it has nothing but sublime moments. The essayist wants to hold the balance; and if he is apt to neglect the sublimities of life, it is because he is apt to think that they can take care of themselves; and that if there is the joy of adventure, the thrill of the start in the fresh air of the morning, the rapture of ardent companionship, the gladness of the arrival, yet there must be long spaces in between, when the pilgrim jogs steadily along, and seems to come no nearer to the spire on the horizon or to the shining embanked cloud land of the West. He has nothing then but his own thoughts to help him, unless he is alert to see what is happening in hedgerow and copse, and the work of the essayist is to make some-thing rich and strange of those seemingly monotonous spaces, those lengths of level road.

Is, then, the Essay in literature a thing which simply stands outside classification, like Argon among the elements, of which the only thing which can be predicated is that it is there? Or like Justice in Plato's Republic, a thing which the talkers set out to define, and which ends by being the one thing left in a state when the definable qualities are taken away? No, it is not that. It is rather like what is called an organ prelude, a little piece with a theme, not very strict perhaps in form, but which can be fancifully treated, modulated from, and colored at will. It is a little criticism of life at some one point clearly enough defined.

We may follow any mood, we may look at life in fifty different ways—the only thing we must not do is to despise or deride, out of ignorance or prejudice, the influences which affect others; because the essence of all experience is that we should perceive something which we do not begin by knowing, and learn that life has a fullness and a richness in all sorts of diverse ways which we do not at first even dream of suspecting.

The essayist, then, is in his particular fashion an interpreter of life, a critic of life. He does not see life as the historian, or as the philosopher, or as the poet, or as the novelist, and yet he has a touch of all these. He is not concerned with discovering a theory of it all, or fitting the various parts of it into each other. He works rather on what is called the analytic method, observing, recording, interpreting, just as things strike him, and letting his fancy play over their beauty and significance; the end of it all being this: that he is deeply concerned with the charm and quality of things, and desires to put it all in the clearest and gentlest light, so that at least he may make others love life a little better, and prepare them for its infinite variety and alike for its joyful and mournful surprises.

On Inspiration

John Pfannkuchen

As a person who never knows what to do, or when to do it, I am always envious of the passionate and resolute poet, artist, film maker, or musician, struck by a bolt of inspiration, toiling away into the little hours, with sweat working down their brow, as their fingers cramp and their back twists, sacrificing joyfully their bodies to bring to the world some vision. It seems that rather the vision is in control, and doing all the work, rather than the artist—yet it's the artist that gets all the credit!

That looks easy, or at least fun, I say to myself. What's wrong with me, that I'd rather lie on the couch very still, and watch my feet, like little headstones rising from the cushion? I wonder to myself where can inspiration be got? Do they sell it at the gas station, in little bottles beside the card machine, along with five hour energy drinks and sticks of bubblegum? I've tried everything on that counter individually and in horrible combination. The result was jittery steps, a sore jaw, and an overwhelming feeling of spearmint. But alas, no inspiration.

Sometimes I will sit down at a cafe and think to myself, "Now is the time to be productive. Now is the time to write, or draw, or to do… something!"

What I usually do is berate myself. "Listen, self," I say, "Why are you so lazy? What's wrong with you?" I imagine the accomplished writers in their mid 40s, the young progenies, the towering legends, all my heroes, Shakespeare, for crying out loud, all of their eyes glowing in the darkness, hovering above me, pressing down on me. Soon I can't breathe properly, it feels stuffy, warm, my inability to move feels like a sin, and so I stand and move to my desk, slowly, and shamefully. Because, you see dear reader, the guilt of the writer is two-fold, you feel guilty for not writing, but when you try to write, you feel guilty for not writing well enough.

So I finally lift the desk a pen, heavy as iron chains, and manage to hold it over a piece of parchment, and heaving it left and right, make some scant forms resembling symbols, which may or may not convey sounds that, when combined create words in our language—every single one of those phantoms sneer, laugh, jeer, heckle and shout; a din of frothing geniuses and progenies and heroes, cruel and contemptuous, and well—not very friendly.

One has to have the gull to sit at that desk and endure it. One has to have resilience. How this strength comes about I do not know. I have some tips for managing the process, however, because I will tell you a secret, though it may seem obvious once I reveal it. The secret is this: once you begin writing, and rewriting, and rearranging, and reading, and rereading, and editing, you'll find that the horrible din subsides, dies down, fades into the background. It's never totally gone, at least not for long—but it becomes a part of the white noise that is the writing process. You learn to drown it out with the sounds of your own toil. Never mind the geniuses, you say to yourself, I have work to do.

But it's just getting started that is so hard! In fact the harder I try to start, the less inspired I feel. But never mind that, I pick up my pen and I begin. My philosophy is that, if I am to be a bad writer, then so be it. I shall write badly—but productively. That is, I will get all the bad, stupid, cliché, hackneyed words, thoughts and ideas onto the page, quickly and with as little fanfare as possible, so that once it's done and out of me, hopefully I can pan some gold from the silt. I start a list. I write down all of the obvious stuff. All the droll and boring and useless stuff. Everything—everything I can think of. I get it onto the page. And once I've exhausted these things I keep going, finding more and more, pushing myself, until eventually I hit oil, or scratch through the skin and draw blood—here is something truly stupid, I think, but hey—something no one has thought of. It's stupid, but it's not cliché, or obvious, or hackneyed. It's original stupidity, and that's something.

That's how I discovered the humble list. I find lists easy to write, and it takes less time to make changes to a list than to a finished draft. Once I really get going, and start branching out into different kinds of lists, they become extensions of my thoughts and memories. It seems the more I use lists to remember and brainstorm, the longer my lists become, and the better I get at using them.

Sometimes, when I want to respond to an article, or some aggravating thing someone has said to me (without getting my ticket punched, as it were), I compose a list of impressions, getting down all the things one cannot say in polite society.

Once that ugly business is concluded I move onto a slightly neater, if not uglier business—dissecting the original source. I begin by sorting the original argument into a few "take away" points. I list all of the major points, topics, or issues that composed my first impressions. I don't impose any kind of order or priority of any kind, because I know the moment I start forcing myself to organize the whole thing this art will feel like work, and then I'll end up where I began—on the couch. I tell myself that later, when my muse finally visits me, I can jumble everything around and reorder it without consequence.

Then I embellish my lists without removing anything. And if I should notice or think of something new, or make a connections, they are added to the list. Only when I feel I have written the world's most complete list do I begin forming whole sentences—comprised of thoughts, observations and impressions onto the items. I especially like to dwell on the combination of thoughts which are closely related. With these lists I can then plan more research, and from this research I can spin out more lists.

When you can't wait forever for inspiration to come to you, try making observations and writing down lists. Lists, lists, lists!

On the Illness of My Muse

Hilaire Belloc

The other day I noticed that my Muse, who had long been ailing, silent and morose, was showing signs of actual illness.

Now, though it is by no means one of my habits to coddle the dogs, cats and other familiars of my household, yet my Muse had so pitiful an appearance that I determined to send for the doctor, but not before I had seen her to bed with a hot bottle, a good supper, and such other comforts as the Muses are accustomed to value. All that could be done for the poor girl was done thoroughly; a fine fire was lit in her bedroom, and a great number of newspapers such as she is given to reading for her recreation were bought at a neighboring shop. When she had drunk her wine and read in their entirety the Daily Telegraph, the Morning Post, the Standard, the Daily Mail, the Daily Express, the Times, the Daily News, and even the Advertiser, I was glad to see her sink into a profound slumber.

I will confess that the jealousy which is easily aroused among servants when one of their number is treated with any special courtesy gave me some concern, and I was at the pains of explaining to the household not only the grave indisposition from which the Muse suffered, but also the obligation I was under to her on account of her virtues: which were, her long and faithful service, her willingness, and the excess of work which she had recently been compelled to perform. Her fellow-servants, to my astonishment and pleasure, entered at once into the spirit of my apology: the still-room maid offered to sit up with her all night, or at least until the trained nurse should arrive, and the groom of the chambers, with a good will that I confess was truly surprising in one of his proud nature, volunteered to go himself and order straw for the street from a neighboring stable.

The cause of this affection which the Muse had aroused in the whole household I subsequently discovered to lie in her own amiable and unselfish temper. She had upon two occasions inspired the knife-boy to verses which had subsequently appeared in the Spectator, and with weekly regularity she would lend her aid to the cook in the composition of those technical reviews by which (as it seemed) that domestic increased her ample wages.

The Muse had slept for a full six hours when the doctor arrived—a specialist in these matters and one who has before now been called in (I am proud to say) by such great persons as Mr. Hichens, Mr. Churchill, and Mr. Roosevelt when their Muses have been out of sorts. Indeed, he is that doctor who operated for aphasia upon the Muse of the late Mr. Rossetti just before his demise. His fees are high, but I was willing enough to pay, and certainly would never have consented—as have, I regret to say, so many of my unworthy contemporaries—to employ a veterinary surgeon upon such an occasion.

The great specialist approached with a determined air the couch where the patient lay, awoke her according to the ancient formula, and proceeded to question her upon her symptoms. He soon discovered their gravity, and I could see by his manner that he was anxious to an extreme. The Muse had grown so weak as to be unable to dictate even a little blank verse, and the indisposition had so far affected her mind that she had no memory of Parnassus, but deliriously maintained that she had been born in the home counties—nay, in the neighborhood of Uxbridge. Her every phrase was a deplorable commonplace, and, on the physician applying a stethoscope and begging her to attempt some verse, she could give us nothing better than a sonnet upon the expansion of the Empire. Her weakness was such that she could do no more than awake, and that feebly, while she professed herself totally unable to arise, to expand, to soar, to haunt, or to perform any of those exercises which are proper to her profession.

When his examination was concluded the doctor took me aside and asked me upon what letters the patient had recently fed. I told him upon the daily Press, some of the reviews, the telegrams from the latest seat of war, and occasionally a debate in Parliament. At this he shook his head and asked whether too much had not recently been asked of her. I admitted that she had done a very considerable amount of work for so young a Muse in the past year, though its quality was doubtful, and I hastened to add that I was the less to blame as she had wasted not a little of her powers upon others without asking my leave; notably upon the knife-boy and the cook.

The doctor was then good enough to write out a prescription in Latin and to add such general recommendations as are commonly of more value than physic. She was to keep her bed, to be allowed no modern literature of any kind, unless Milton and Swift may be admitted as moderns, and even these authors and their predecessors were to be admitted in very sparing quantities. If any signs of inversion, archaism, or neologistic tendencies appeared he was to be summoned at once; but of these (he added) he had little fear. He did not doubt that in a few weeks we should have her up and about again, but he warned me against letting her begin work too soon.

"I would not," he said, "permit her to undertake any effort until she can inspire within one day of twelve hours at least eighteen quatrains, and those lucid, grammatical, and moving. As for single lines, tags, fine phrases, and the rest, they are no sign whatever of returning health, if anything of the contrary."

He also begged that she might not be allowed any Greek or Latin for ten days, but I reassured him upon the matter by telling him that she was totally unacquainted with those languages—at which he expressed some pleasure but even more astonishment.

At last he told me that he was compelled to be gone; the season had been very hard, nor had he known so general a breakdown among the Muses of his various clients.

I thought it polite as I took him to the door to ask after some of his more distinguished patients; he was glad to say that the Archbishop of Armagh's was very vigorous indeed, in spite of the age of her illustrious master. He had rarely known a more inventive or courageous female, but when, as I handed him into his carriage, I asked after that of Mr. Kipling, his face became suddenly grave; and he asked me, "Have you not heard?"

"No," said I; but I had a fatal presentiment of what was to follow, and indeed I was almost prepared for it when he answered in solemn tones:

"She is dead."

Free Write

John Pfannkuchen

Whenever I begin writing there is some anxiety about what or how to write. I have tried thinking more, drawing detailed outlines, staring at walls, and pounding desks to be of little use. It turns out that, for me at least that my own thinking can get in the way of writing.

When I find myself working on something complex, that has a lot of moving parts, I tend to feel torn between one part of a project and another, or one stage of composition and a later stage. I have found that my mind spends a surprising amount of time planning, predicting, and imagining--sometimes without my noticing, until I realize I've been working for hours and have nothing to show for it!

What if it's this awareness of ourselves, and the process, that stops us dead in our tracks? So I've decided that in my case thinking and worrying too much may be the problem. The most confounding, and yet most obvious fact, about thinking too much is that the one thing that cannot solve it is more thinking.

So what's the obvious answer? Well, to think less, I suppose. But how am I supposed to write without thinking? So here's a technique that I draw on nowadays, that was shown to me in college creative writing classes. I find it works wonders for turning the brain off and just accomplishing a draft quickly.

Instead of just thinking about my topic, I give myself some sort of object to focus on. It can be a photograph, or place to write about from my thoughts, recordings or observations.

Then I put my pen to the paper and start just writing any old thing that comes to mind about the object. Once my pen is moving, I must keep it moving at all costs; recording everything—and anything. Even if it's nonsense, circular, or just observations regarding the room. I do not stop to read what I have written. I do not erase anything. I do not correct mistakes of grammar or spelling. I remind myself that revision can be done after the session is over. When I write in this manner I do nothing but transfer words from thin air to the page, banishing my mind from the process.

Of course it goes without saying that working in a quiet environment (or one filled with white noise), with no video games, powered smart phones, friends, relatives, cats, dogs, parakeets, or nosy strangers is a must. I'll go to my room, or find a spot in a cafe and if a friendly person should look about ready to say something to me, or ask me what I'm up to, I scowl at them—trying to look very serious and busy. Don't bother me I project, I need to get this done!

For the aspiring free writer I would say that the greatest asset of free writing is its simplicity. One must empty their mind, and even though an essayist may be distracted at first, she should continue writing until all distractions have melted away, then continue writing for as long as she can. She will know when it is time to rest. Her timer will ring, her hand will start to cramp. She can take a minute and rest, get up and walk around, then come back and look at what's been written. Then the essayist must ask: is there no more I can add? Some detail I missed?

After, if I feel as though I have written in a shallow manner, I look back at the writing. It's not unusual that I am left with a sense of dread about the quality of the writing this technique produces, yet it usually reads better than I think it would. I think this dread are the phantoms in my head lashing out at me for sending them to the corner while I got work done, like petulant children. But if the work I produce truly is as bad as I suspect, I simply ask myself if there's anything I can do with the ideas that are there.

Here's something else I do: I use lists to guide my free writing. What I'll do is create a loose outline out of lists, and then free write between the points of the list. I use each point as a free writing prompt, focusing like a laser on just that small part of the work. If my free writing causes me to ask new questions, then I do additional research!

If this writing and additional research changes everything about my argument, then I update my lists as I work.

Here's another form of writing that I do. It's called free association. What I do is look at points in your lists, and choose a word there. What is the first thing I imagine? Whatever it is, I write that thing down, and describe it using my imagination.

Consider this: what do you see when you read the "storm"? Do you picture a cloud? A flash of lightning? Perhaps a flooded sewer drain, or a tree bent over in the wind? Whatever you imagine, that is what you associated first with the word "storm." Perhaps you're a visual person, and imagined more than one thing. Perhaps you imagined a whole scene. Write what you saw down as quickly as you can. Everything, leaving nothing out. Did you hear rolling thunder? Did you feel the cold rain falling upon your arms? Did you breathe the dust, swept in a wind from the spring thaw? Whatever you imagined, begin there.

Now either go back to the last word you free wrote about, or choose another word. Repeat the entire process over again. This is called "looping" by some, but "writing associatively" by others. Writing by association is effective because as we write we encode our experiences with language. Language is all interconnected within our culture, just like our memories and thoughts.

I like to think that our imaginations are a small part of a bigger network. This network is shared with everyone who speaks the same language. What makes this interesting is that we all have different experiences, and the experiences we do share are never encoded in exactly the same way. Which is why when I read about familiar experiences they seem new and interesting. I've decided that that's how reading can build empathy, and allow us to "broaden" our minds. We're just gaining access to more and more of the big net that is our shared experience.

So regardless of how one associates the word "storm." Someone out there will be touched, surprised, or bewildered by the associations. I believe that's a good thing.

On the Pleasure of Taking Up One's Pen

Hilaire Belloc

Among the sadder and smaller pleasures of this world I count this pleasure: the pleasure of taking up one's pen.

It has been said by very many people that there is a tangible pleasure in the mere act of writing: in choosing and arranging words. It has been denied by many. It is affirmed and denied in the life of Doctor Johnson, and for my part I would say that it is very true in some rare moods and wholly false in most others. However, of writing and the pleasure in it I am not writing here (with pleasure), but of the pleasure of taking up one's pen, which is quite another matter.

Note what the action means. You are alone. Even if the room is crowded (as was the smoking-room in the G.W.R. Hotel, at Paddington, only the other day, when I wrote my "Statistical Abstract of Christendom"), even if the room is crowded, you must have made yourself alone to be able to write at all. You must have built up some kind of wall and isolated your mind. You are alone, then; and that is the beginning.

If you consider at what pains men are to be alone: how they climb mountains, enter prisons, profess monastic vows, put on eccentric daily habits, and seclude themselves in the garrets of a great town, you will see that this moment of taking up the pen is not least happy in the fact that then, by a mere association of ideas, the writer is alone.

So much for that. Now not only are you alone, but you are going to "create".

When people say "create" they flatter themselves. No man can create anything. I knew a man once who drew a horse on a bit of paper to amuse the company and covered it all over with many parallel streaks as he drew. When he had done this, an aged priest (present upon that occasion) said, "You are pleased to draw a zebra." When the priest said this the man began to curse and to swear, and to protest that he had never seen or heard of a zebra. He said it was all done out of his own head, and he called heaven to witness, and his patron saint (for he was of the Old English Territorial Catholic Families—his patron saint was Aethelstan), and the salvation of his immortal soul he also staked, that he was as innocent of zebras as the babe unborn. But there! He persuaded no one, and the priest scored. It was most evident that the Territorial was crammed full of zebraical knowledge.

All this, then, is a digression, and it must be admitted that there is no such thing as a man's "creating". But anyhow, when you take up your pen you do something devilish pleasing: there is a prospect before you. You are going to develop a germ: I don't know what it is, and I promise you I won't call it creation—but possibly a god is creating through you, and at least you are making believe at creation. Anyhow, it is a sense of mastery and of origin, and you know that when you have done, something will be added to the world, and little destroyed. For what will you have destroyed or wasted? A certain amount of white paper at a farthing a square yard (and I am not certain it is not pleasanter all diversified and variegated with black wriggles)—a certain amount of ink meant to be spread and dried: made for no other purpose. A certain infinitesimal amount of quill—torn from the silly goose for no purpose whatsoever but to minister to the high needs of Man.

Here you cry "Affectation! Affectation! How do I know that the fellow writes with a quill? A most unlikely habit!" To that I answer you are right. Less assertion, please, and more humility. I will tell you frankly with what I am writing. I am writing with a Waterman's Ideal Fountain Pen. The nib is of pure gold, as was the throne of Charlemagne, in the "Song of Roland." That throne (I need hardly tell you) was borne into Spain across the cold and awful passes of the Pyrenees by no less than a hundred and twenty mules, and all the Western world adored it, and trembled before it when it was set up at every halt under pine trees, on the upland grasses. For he sat upon it, dreadful and commanding: there weighed upon him two centuries of age; his brows were level with justice and experience, and his beard was so tangled and full, that he was called "bramble-bearded Charlemagne." You have read how, when he stretched out his hand at evening, the sun stood still till he had found the body of Roland? No? You must read about these things.

Well then, the pen is of pure gold, a pen that runs straight away like a willing horse, or a jolly little ship; indeed, it is a pen so excellent that it reminds me of my subject: the pleasure of taking up one's pen.

God bless you, pen! When I was a boy, and they told me work was honorable, useful, cleanly, sanitary, wholesome, and necessary to the mind of man, I paid no more attention to them than if they had told me that public men were usually honest, or that pigs could fly. It seemed to me that they were merely saying silly things they had been told to say. Nor do I doubt to this day that those who told me these things at school were but preaching a dull and careless round. But now I know that the things they told me were true. God bless you, pen of work, pen of drudgery, pen of letters, pen of posings, pen rabid, pen ridiculous, pen glorified. Pray, little pen, be worthy of the love I bear you, and consider how noble I shall make you some day, when you shall live in a glass case with a crowd of tourists round you every day from 10 to 4; pen of justice, pen of the saeva indignatio, pen of majesty and of light. I will write with you some day a considerable poem; it is a compact between you and me. If I cannot make one of my own, then I will write out some other man's; but you, pen, come what may, shall write out a good poem before you die, if it is only the Allegro.

The pleasure of taking up one's pen has also this, peculiar among all pleasures, that you have the freedom to lay it down when you will. Not so with love. Not so with victory. Not so with glory.

Had I begun the other way round, I would have called this Work, "The Pleasure of laying down one's Pen." But I began it where I began it, and I am going on to end it just where it is going to end.

What other occupation, avocation, dissertation, or intellectual recreation can you cease at will? Not bridge—you go on playing to win. Not public speaking—they ring a bell. Not mere converse—you have to answer everything the other insufficient person says. Not life, for it is wrong to kill one's self; and as for the natural end of living, that does not come by one's choice; on the contrary, it is the most capricious of all accidents.

But the pen you lay down when you will. At any moment: without remorse, without anxiety, without dishonor, you are free to do this dignified and final thing (I am just going to do it)... You lay it down.

Observation Through a Lens

John Pfannkuchen

Sometimes I like to imagine having a pair of glasses with dozens of different colored lenses. Each pair of lenses, when popped into the frame, "filter out" objects, people, or actions so that I can only see certain types of things.

I'll pop on a pair of "historical lenses," and look at the buildings around, removing everything newer than 1835. What is left? Some old rail road tracks, main street and front street and River Row, and a few buildings that today are crumbling but were brand new almost 200 years ago. I take some notes.

Then I'll pop in my aesthetic lenses, and find out what are the main colors, are the shapes sharp, dull, liquid, flowing, or harsh? Are the patterns geometric, or calico? What's the atmosphere? What's the mood? Why? Then I make a list.

Then I begin to wonder about nature, and put on my ecosystem lens, and observe the weather, the season, the geography—atop a mountain, or at the foot of an ocean? This leads me to my economic lenses, dealing with currency and consumers—the machinations and movements of mankind, as a means of production and the like, of buying and selling. When everything is stripped away human interaction becomes a series of transactions, and I can see the transfer of wealth and power. Reminded of power, I reach for my sociological lenses, and wonder how do these people relate to each other? Are some rich, or some poor? Husband or wife? Politicians or outcasts?

Then I take a step back, and think about the hidden systems of meaning—the symbols, metaphor and analogy—of parallels and comparisons, I watch for the words of power, logos, hand signs, gestures, movements of eye and mouth that "stand in" for other things, like place-holders. When I see something mysterious I wonder: what else could this mean?

By using my lenses I am discovering my topic by figuring out what interests me. In the last task, what lens did I write the most about? This is an indicator to me of what I'll probably be writing about. I find it's always best to follow my interests and curiosity, instead of what may seem the easiest topic. When I am truly interested the essay writes itself. But writing about something I think will be easier? Easier but boring topics typically result in writing that strikes me as dull. As my enthusiasm falls ill, and my muse is nowhere to be found, I wonder if the reader might feel the same.

Ideas

Arthur Benson

There are certain great ideas which, if we have any intelligence and thoughtfulness at all, we cannot help coming across the track of, just as when we walk far into the deep country, in the time of the blossoming of flowers, we step for a moment into a waft of fragrance, cast upon the air from orchard or thicket or scented field of bloom.

These ideas are very various in quality; some of them deliciously haunting and transporting, some grave and solemn, some painfully sad and strong. Some of them seem to hint at unseen beauty and joy, some have to do with problems of conduct and duty, some with the relation in which we wish to stand or are forced to stand with other human beings; some are questionings born of grief and pain, what the meaning of sorrow is, whether pain has a further intention, whether the spirit survives the life which is all that we can remember of existence; but the strange thing about all these ideas is that we find them suddenly in the mind and soul; we do not seem to invent them, though we cannot trace them; and even if we find them in books that we read or words that we hear, they do not seem wholly new to us; we recognize them as things that we have dimly felt and perceived, and the reason why they often have so mysterious an effect upon us is that they seem to take us outside of ourselves, further back than we can recollect, beyond the faint horizon, into something as wide and great as the illimitable sea or the depths of sunset sky.

Some of these ideas have to do with the constitution of society, the combined and artificial peace in which human beings live, and then they are political ideas; or they deal with such things as numbers, curves, classes of animals and plants, the soil of the earth, the changes of the seasons, the laws of weight and mass, and then they are scientific ideas; some have to do with right and wrong conduct, actions and qualities, and then they are religious or ethical ideas. But there is a class of thoughts which belong precisely to none of these things, but which are concerned with the perception of beauty, in forms and colors, musical sounds, human faces and limbs, words majestic or sweet; and this sense of beauty may go further, and may be discerned in qualities, regarded not from the point of view of their rightness and justice, but according as they are fine and noble, evoking our admiration and our desire; and these are poetical ideas.

It is not of course possible exactly to classify ideas, because there is a great overlapping of them and a wide interchange. The thought of the slow progress of man from something rude and beast like, the statement of the astronomer about the swarms of worlds swimming in space, may awaken the sense of poetry which is in its essence the sense of wonder. I shall not attempt in these few pages to limit and define the sense of poetry. I shall merely attempt to describe the kind of effect it has or may have in life, what our relation is or may be to it, what claim it may be said to have upon us, whether we can practice it, and whether we ought to do so.

On Paragraphs

John Pfannkuchen

Imagine a wall, like those of a prison, or of a skyscraper, or standing at the base of the Hoover Dam (with the water drained, of course). Whenever I stand next to a very large wall, I am made to feel all the more small, and I imagine horrible things, like the wall collapsing upon me. This is the same feeling I get from looking at a page of text that has no paragraphs. It feels imposing, and I have a hard time getting myself to begin. I think humans have a hard time reading walls of text. For me, it is easy for my eyes to become lost among the text. Aside from its imposing nature, the wall of text gives me no sense of meaning, no context. It is the whiteness of the whale; the blackness of night—it is bleak and meaningless and fills me with dread. On the other than, shorter paragraphs comfort me with the notion that there is an end and a beginning, and armed with a sense of what's in store, I begin merrily, knowing feeling some sense of progress and accomplishment with the completion of each paragraph.

A divided piece of writing, in which the author has a natural feel for when to hit the Enter (Return) key, flows like a familiar song, giving the work a sense of rhythm, as do the words and sentences that make them up.

Even better are paragraphs that are topical in nature, that is, broken up into the smallest possible subtopics. To quote William Strunk, the Cornell professor who authored the original Elements of Style:

"A subject requires subdivision into topics, each of which should be made the subject of a paragraph. The object of treating each topic in a paragraph by itself is, of course, to aid the reader. The beginning of each paragraph is a signal to him that a new step in the development of the subject has been reached."

And as a writer myself, I find that crafting paragraphs, at first, isn't so hard. Paragraphing can be done along the way, especially if the essayist is experienced and has a firm grasp of what they are saying, or if they're following an outline. If, however, the writer has little sense of what the finished product will look like, they can always reset the paragraphs upon revision, rereading and deciding what stays, what goes, and how to organize the rest.

Using well defined, topical paragraphs is more than just an aid for readers, however. As an essayist it allows me to do magical things within the revision process, especially if I am working on a computer: I can merely pick up a subtopic in the form of a paragraph and move it around, without making a mess of things, assuming the paragraphs are self contained and somewhat modular in nature.

However, a question I often struggle with is, after the paragraphs are in the most effective order, whether to add some sort of transition between them, or leave them in a minimalist fashion, asking the reader to make the leap on their own...?

An Essay On Essays

Katharine Fullerton Gerould

Some of the rhetoric books my generation used in college went back to Aristotle for many of their definitions. "Rhetoric," he says, "may be defined as a faculty of discovering all the possible means of persuasion in any subject." Persuasion, indeed, is the purpose of the essay more so than of fiction or poetry, since the essay deals always with an idea. No essay is truly an essay, regardless of how unfocused or informal it is, unless it states a proposition for the reader to accept. Though it be only the defense of a mood, subject and predicate are the bare bones of any essay. It may be of a complex nature (like many of Emerson's) stating several propositions; but unless it states at least one proposition, it is not an essay. It may be a dream or a poem, but I repeat, it is not an essay.

Let us neglect the old rhetorical differences between exposition [story narrative] and argument. To sort all essays into those two types of writing would be more troublesome a task than any task a wicked stepmother gave to her stepdaughter in a fairy-tale. We can no more do it without the help of magic than could the poor princess. When is an essay argument, and when is it exposition—who knows?

Regardless, in so far as the essay attempts to persuade, it partakes of the nature of argument. Yet who would call Lamb's "Dream Children" an argument? Or who shall say it is not an essay? It contains a proposition, if you will only look for it; yet to associate Lamb's persuading process with the forum would be preposterous. All writing presupposes an audience (which some of our younger writers seem to forget) but formal argument presupposes opponents, and I cannot find the faintest scent of an enemy at hand in "Dream Children."

Let us now forget the rhetoricians, and use our own words (our common sense too, if we have any). Let us say, first, that the purpose of the essay is persuasion; and that the essay states a proposition. Indeed, we need to be as rigorously simple as that, if we are going to consider briefly a type that is supposed to include Bacon's "Of Truth," De Quincey's "Murder as a Fine Art," Lamb's "In Praise of Chimney Sweeps," Hazlitt's "On Going a Journey," Irving's "Bachelors," Hunt's "Getting up on Cold Mornings," Poe's "The Poetic Principle," Emerson's "Self-Reliance," Arnold's "Function of Criticism," Stevenson's "Penny Plain and Twopence Colored," Paul Elmer More's "The Demon of the Absolute," Chesterton's "On Leisure," Max Beerbohm's "No. 2. The Pines," Stephen Leacock's "People We Know," and James Truslow Adams' "The Mucker Pose."

The foregoing list, in itself, confesses our main difficulty in delimiting the essay. The most popular kind of essay, perhaps, is that known as "familiar." When people deplore the passing of the essay from the pages of our magazines, it is usually this that they are regretting. They are thinking wistfully of pieces of prose like Lamb's "Sarah Battle on Whist," Leigh Hunt's "The Old Gentleman," Stevenson's "El Dorado," Max Beerbohm's "Mobled King." They mean the essay that is largely descriptive, more or less sentimental or humorous, in which it is sometimes difficult to find a stated proposition. This kind of prose has not been very popular since [World War I], and I for one, am not regretting it. It will come back—as long as the ghost of Montaigne is permitted to revisit the glimpses of the moon. But the familiar-essay-which-is-hardly-an-essay can be spared for a few years if necessary, since it demands literary gifts of a very high order, and the authors mentioned have at present no competitors in this field. If the bones of the essay are to be weak, the flesh must be exceeding fair and firm.

Are we to admit, at all, that "Sarah Battle" and "The Old Gentleman," and "El Dorado" and "Mobled King" are essays? Do they state a proposition to which they attempt to persuade us? Well, we can twist them to a proposition, if we are very keen on our definition—though I think most of us would admit that they are chiefly descriptive and that they are only gently directed to the creation of opinion. Must we then deny that they are essays? No, I think they are essays, though it is obvious that the familiar essayist goes about his business far otherwise than Arnold or Emerson or Macaulay. He attempts rather to sharpen our perceptions than to convince us of a statement; to win our sympathy rather than our suffrage. His proposition is less important to him than his mood. If put to it, we can sift a proposition out of each one of these—and they were especially chosen because they put our definition on its defense. Lamb states, if you like, that to abide by the rigor of the game is in its way an admirable thing; Leigh Hunt states, if you like, that growing old is a melancholy business; Stevenson states that it is better to travel hopefully than to arrive; Max Beerbohm states that no man is worthy to be reproduced as a statue. But the author's proposition, in such essays, is not our main interest. This brings us to another consideration which may clarify the matter.

Though an essay must state a proposition, there are other requirements to be fulfilled. The bones of subject and predicate must be clothed in a certain way. The basis of the essay is meditation, and it must in a measure admit the reader to the meditative process. (This procedure is frankly hinted in all those titles that used to begin with "Of" or "On": "Of Truth," "Of Riches," "On the Graces and Anxieties of Pig-Driving," "On the Knocking at the Gate in 'Macbeth'," "On the Enjoyment of Unpleasant Places"). An essay, to some extent, thinks aloud; though not in the loose and pointless way to which the "stream of consciousness" addicts have accustomed us. The author must have made up his mind—otherwise, where is his proposition? But the essay, I think, should show how and why he made up his mind as he did; should engagingly rehearse the steps by which he came to his conclusions. ("Francis of Verulam reasoned thus with himself.") Meditation; but an oriented and fruitful meditation.

This is the most intimate of forms, because it permits you to see a mind at work. On the quality and temper of that mind depends the goodness of the production. Now, if the essay is essentially meditative, it cannot be polemical. No one, I think, would call Cicero's first oration against Catiline an essay; or Burke's Speech on the Conciliation of America; hardly more could we call Swift's "Modest Proposal" a true essay. The author must have made up his mind, but when he has made it up with a vengeance, he will not produce an essay. Because the process is meditative, the manner should be courteous; he should always, by implication, admit that there are good people who may not agree with him; his irony should never turn to the sardonic. Reasonableness, urbanity (as Matthew Arnold would have said) are prerequisites for a form whose temper is meditative rather than polemical.

We have said that this is the most intimate of forms. Not only for technical reasons, though obviously the essayist is less sharply controlled by his structure than the dramatist or the sonneteer or even the novelist. It is the most intimate because it is the most subjective. When people talk of "creative" and "critical" writing—dividing all literature thus—they always call the essay critical. In spite of Oscar Wilde, to call it critical is probably correct; for creation implies objectivity. The created thing, though the author have torn its raw substance from his very vitals, ends by being separate from its creator. The essay, however, is incurably subjective.

A lot of criticism is more delightful than the prose or verse that is being criticized. It is nonetheless criticism. Wilde is to some extent right when he says that criticism is the only civilized form of autobiography; but he is not so right when he says that the highest criticism is more creative than creation. All Bacon's essays together but build up a portrait of Bacon reasoning with himself; and what is the substance of the Essays of Elia, but Elia? "Subjective" is the word, however, rather than "creative."

It is this subjectivity that has confused many minds. It is subjectivity run wild that has tempted many people to believe that the familiar essay alone is the essay; which would make some people contend that an essay does not necessarily state a proposition. But we are talking of the essay itself; not of those bits of whimsical prose which are to the true essay what expanded anecdote is to the short story.

The essay, then, having persuasion for its object, states a proposition; its method is meditation; it is subjective rather than objective, critical rather than creative. It can never be a mere marshaling of facts; for it struggles, in one way or another, for truth; and truth is something one arrives at by the help of facts, not the facts themselves. Meditating on facts may bring one to truth; facts alone will not. Nor can there be an essay without a point of view and a personality. A geometrical proposition cannot be an essay, since, though it arranges facts in a certain pattern, there is involved no personal meditative process, conditioned by the individuality of the author. A geometrical proposition is not subjective. One is even tempted to say that its tone is not urbane!

Perhaps—with the essay thus defined—we shall understand without effort why it is being so little written at present. The whole world is living more or less in a state of war; and a state of war produces any literary form more easily than the essay. It is not hard to see why. People in a state of war, whether the war be military or economic, express themselves polemically. A wise man said to me, many years ago, that, in his opinion, the worst by-product of the World War was propaganda. Many times, in the course of the years, I have had occasion to recall that statement. There are perhaps times and places where propaganda is justified—it is not for me to say. But I think we should all agree that the increasing habit of using the technique of propaganda is corrupting the human mind in its most secret and delicate processes. Propaganda has, in common with all other expression, the object of persuasion; but it pursues that legitimate object by illegitimate means—by suggestio falsi and suppressio veri; by the argumentum ad hominem and hitting below the belt; by demagogic appeal and the disregard of right reason. The victim of propaganda is not intellectually persuaded, but intellectually—if not emotionally—coerced. The essayist, whatever the limitations of his intelligence, is bound over to be honest; the propagandist is always dishonest.

To qualify a large number of the articles and pseudo-essays that appear at present in our serious periodicals, British and American, as "dishonest" calls for a little explaining. When one says that the propagandist is always dishonest, one means this: He is a man so convinced of the truth of a certain proposition that he dissembles the facts that tell against it. Occasionally, he is dishonest through ignorance—he is verily unaware of any facts save those that argue for him. Sometimes, having approached his subject with his decision already made, he is unable to appreciate the value of hostile facts, even though he is aware of them. In the latter case, instead of presenting those hostile facts fairly, he tends to suppress or distort them because he is afraid that his audience, readers or listeners, will not react to them precisely as he has done. The propagandist believes (when he is not a paid prostitute) that his conclusions are right; but, no more than any other demagogue, does he like to give other men and women a fair chance to decide for themselves. The last thing he will show them is Francis of Verulam reasoning with himself. He cannot encourage the meditative process. He is, at best, the special pleader.

It can have escaped no reader of British and American periodicals that there is very little urbane meditation going on in print. Half the articles published are propaganda—political, economic, social; the other half are purely informational, mere catalogs of fact. The essay is nowhere. Either there is no proposition, or evidence is suppressed. Above all, there is no meditation—no urbanity. All this is characteristic of the state of war in which we are unfortunately living; that state of war which, alas! Permits us few unprejudiced hours.

Yet I think many people would agree that we need those unprejudiced hours rather particularly, just now. We need the essay rather particularly, just now, since fiction and poetry have suffered even more cruelly than critical prose from the corruption of propaganda on the one hand and the rage for "fact-finding" on the other. We need to get away from polemics; we even need to get away from statistics. Granted that we are in a state of war: are we positively so badly off that we must permit every sense save the economic to be atrophied; that we cannot afford to think about life in any terms except those of bread?

The desperate determination to guarantee bread to every one—which seems to be the basis of all our political and economic quarreling—is perhaps our major duty. And after? As the French say. Is it not worth our while to keep ourselves complex and civilized, so that, when bread for every one is guaranteed, we shall be capable of entertaining other interests?

The preoccupation with bread alone is a savage's preoccupation; even when it concerns itself altruistically with other people's bread, it is still a savage's preoccupation. The preoccupation with facts to the exclusion of what can be done with them, and the incapacity for logical thinking, are both savage. Until a man begins to think—not merely to lose his temper or to learn by heart—he is, mentally, clothed in the skins of beasts. We are, I fear, under economic stress, de-civilizing ourselves. Between propaganda and "dope" there is little room for the meditative process and the subtler propositions.

I am not urging that we play the flute while Rome burns. I recall the sad entry in Dorothy Wordsworth's journal: "William wasted his mind all day in the magazines." I am not asking the magazines to waste the minds of our Williams....The fact that the familiar essay of the whimsical type is not at the moment popular—that when people wish to be diverted, they prefer Wodehouse to Leacock, let us say—does not disturb me. But it seems a pity that meditative prose should suffer a total eclipse, if only because meditation is highly contagious. A good essay inevitably sets the reader to thinking. Just because it expresses a point of view, is limited by one personality, and cannot be exhaustive or wholly authoritative, it invites the reader to collaboration. A good essay is neither intoxicant nor purge nor anodyne; it is a mental stimulant.

Poetry may be, indeed, as Arnold said, "a criticism of life." But most of us need a different training in critical thinking from that which is offered to us by the poets. A vast amount of the detail of life, detail which preoccupies and concerns us all, is left out of great poetry. We do not spend all our time on the heights, or in the depths, and if we are to live we must reflect on many matters rather temporal than eternal. The essayist says, "Come, let us reason together." That is an invitation—whether given by word of mouth or on the printed page—that civilized people must encourage and, as often as possible in their burdened lives, accept.

On Abstract Language

John Pfannkuchen

One large problem occurs with a writer's logic when she fails to distinguish between the abstract and concrete language. We will first get a clear understanding of the differences between concrete and abstract language. Then we will make our argument use the correct level of abstraction.

Remember that a narrow scope will result in a more precise but less significant argument—and a wide scope will result in a more significant but less precise argument. One way to narrow or widen scope is to double check all the abstraction in our essays.

Abstraction is a purely linguistic phenomenon—that means that it exists only in language.

Ideas, beliefs, events, and processes are abstract. Abstract language often "feels" or seems concrete. But because abstract language cannot be seen or touched this "feeling" of concreteness is not real. However it's not our fault! We confuse abstract and concrete language because the English language treats ideas the same as it does real objects—as nouns. For example:

"The Occurrence at Owl Creek Bridge" is about war.

"The Occurrence at Owl Creek Bridge" takes place on a bridge.

Look at the nouns "war" and "bridge". Can you tell which noun is concrete and which one is abstract? Both words in the above sentences are nouns. I can stand on a bridge—it is a real physical object. However, I cannot go to the store and buy war, I cannot put war in my pocket. But, you say, I can watch a war unfold on my television. There are certain physical objects that come to mind when you think of the act of war. But these physical things are not the act of war. Bombs, guns, tanks, and soldiers. Our minds may associate various concrete objects with ideas. However, war, by itself, is only an idea, and therefor it is an abstraction.

Then what is concrete language? If abstractions are ideas that you cannot experience with the five senses, then concrete things must be just the opposite. Language is said to be concrete if it can be experienced with one or more of the five senses. Concrete language refers to things, objects and people. Physical things. Payton Faruqar, Owl Creek Bridge, a noose, a river, the water—all of these are words that refer to physical objects. As people or objects concrete language refers to physical things.

You'll notice that the specificity and generality of a word plays a role in how abstract or concrete that word is. Words that indicate many things at once, grouped by some kind of logic or characteristic, are called types, stereotypes, classes, or categories. For short I will refer to these as categories. A category in English is language that refers to a collection, class, or type of physical thing. And while the things themselves are concrete, the category, class, or type is abstract. The category is impossible to touch, feel, smell, hear, or see; it is itself an abstract concept. Even though the basis for a category may be a physical quality that certain concrete objects share, such as color, size, or use. This is the "logic of categorization". And regardless of whether it's concrete or abstract in nature, true or false, doesn't matter. Categorical language plays a key role in propaganda and bias—consider a phrase that begins with "all women," or "all Americans" and you'll see what I mean.

One cannot experience a category with any of the five senses—it must be thought of. This marks the difference between the category known simply as saboteur, and a specific saboteur such as Payton Faruqar. When we say that Payton Faruqar is a saboteur, we are really saying that Payton Faruqar belongs to the category of saboteur. But he also belongs to the categories of: man, husband, and victim. But beyond these categories, Payton Faruqar is an individual, unique and independent from his categories—no thing, much less a person, can be summed up by their categories alone.

To expand upon this point, "trees" as a category is somewhat abstract. Many things can be said about "trees" in general, but many more things can be said of certain species of trees (still a category, but slightly less abstract, less general). And what about that particular tree growing in the park? Everything that can be said of all trees, and that tree's specie, can be said of it as well. But one can say more about an individual than its categories implies: what sets it apart from the other trees of its categories? Consider its location, its root structure, its health, its ecosystem and the particular creatures that inhabit it (its internal biomes). These are variables that may or may not be true of other trees like of its species, much the entire category of trees.

After a certain point generalization, and stereotype, fails us. This point is probably most felt in the realm of characterizing the individual human being. The same processes are in play, and a great writer will understand the dangers of abstraction and choose how much abstraction to and not to use in their topic, question, and hypothesis. They will make this choice deliberately--not accidentally. I am always wary of leaving my argument in the hands of a stereotype, or category.

On Them

Hilaire Belloc

I do not like Them. It is no good asking me why, though I have plenty of reasons. I do not like Them. There would be no particular point in saying I do not like Them if it were not that so many people doted on Them, and when one hears Them praised, it goads one to expressing one's hatred and fear of Them.

I know very well that They can do one harm, and that They have occult powers. All the world has known that for a hundred thousand years, more or less, and every attempt has been made to propitiate Them. James I. would drown Their mistress or burn her, but They were spared. Men would mummify Them in Egypt, and worship the mummies; men would carve Them in stone in Cyprus, and Crete and Asia Minor, or (more remarkable still) artists, especially in the Western Empire, would leave Them out altogether; so much was Their influence dreaded. Well, I yield so far as not to print Their name, and only to call Them "They", but I hate Them, and I'm not afraid to say so.

If you will take a little list of the chief crimes that living beings can commit you will find that They commit them all. And They are cruel; cruelty is even in Their tread and expression. They are hatefully cruel. I saw one of Them catch a mouse the other day (the cat is now out of the bag), and it was a very much more sickening sight, I fancy, than ordinary murder. You may imagine that They catch mice to eat them. It is not so. They catch mice to torture them. And what is worse, They will teach this to Their children—Their children who are naturally innocent and fat, and full of goodness, are deliberately and systematically corrupted by Them; there is diabolism in it.

Other beings (I include mankind) will be gluttonous, but gluttonous spasmodically, or with a method, or shamefacedly, or, in some way or another that qualifies the vice; not so They. They are gluttonous always and upon all occasions, and in every place and forever. It was only last Vigil of All Fools' Day when, myself fasting, I filled up the saucer seven times with milk and seven times it was emptied, and there went up the most peevish, querulous, vicious complaint and demand for an eighth. They will eat some part of the food of all that are in the house. Now even a child, the most gluttonous one would think of all living creatures, would not do that. It makes a selection, They do not. They will drink beer. This is not a theory; I know it; I have seen it with my own eyes. They will eat special foods; They will even eat dry bread. Here again I have personal evidence of the fact; They will eat the dog's biscuits, but never upon any occasion will They eat anything that has been poisoned, so utterly lacking are They in simplicity and humility, and so abominably well filled with cunning by whatever demon first brought their race into existence.

They also, alone of all creation, love hateful noises. Some beings indeed (and I count Man among them) cannot help the voice with which they have been endowed, but they know that it is offensive, and are at pains to make it better; others (such as the peacock or the elephant) also know that their cry is unpleasant. They therefore use it sparingly. Others again, the dove, the nightingale, the thrush, know that their voices are very pleasant, and entertain us with them all day and all night long; but They know that Their voices are the most hideous of all the sounds in the world, and, knowing this, They perpetually insist upon thrusting those voices upon us, saying, as it were, "I am giving myself pain, but I am giving you more pain, and therefore I shall go on." And They choose for the place where this pain shall be given, exact and elevated situations, very close to our ears. Is there any need for me to point out that in every city they will begin their wicked jar just at the time when its inhabitants must sleep? In London you will not hear it till after midnight; in the county towns it begins at ten; in remote villages as early as nine.

Their Master also protects them. They have a charmed life. I have seen one thrown from a great height into a London street, which when

It reached it It walked quietly away with the dignity of the Lost World to which It belonged.

If one had the time one could watch Them day after day, and never see Them do a single kind or good thing, or be moved by a single virtuous impulse. They have no gesture for the expression of admiration, love, reverence or ecstasy. They have but one method of expressing content, and They reserve that for moments of physical repletion. The tail, which is in all other animals the signal for joy or for defense, or for mere usefulness, or for a noble anger, is with Them agitated only to express a sullen discontent.

All that They do is venomous, and all that They think is evil, and when I take mine away (as I mean to do next week—in a basket), I shall first read in a book of statistics what is the wickedest part of London, and I shall leave It there, for I know of no one even among my neighbors quite so vile as to deserve such a gift.

On Bias

John Pfannkuchen

Who among us hasn't been asked, at least once, to "choose a thesis, then defend it," or to, "write a thesis driven essay"? When people write this way they usually end up writing propaganda, which is very good for defeating the enemy, but whose truth is questionable at best.

I would say that not all biased writing is propaganda, however. I think the main difference is intention. But that doesn't make it any better, mind you. What do I care, when being misled down a dark and dead-end alleyway, if my guide has ill intentions or is merely incompetent? In either case I have been misled. I suppose the principle thing is bias.

And what is bias? In my opinion it somewhat like, but worse than, the blinders they put on horses. Blinders prevent a horse from being spooked, and running off with the cart, while bias might have the same effect on the reader—preventing the reader from getting up and running away from the writer who chooses only to see and share certain aspects of this world, misrepresenting it and misleading us. Bias blots out things before one's eyes, whereas blinders only obscure the peripheral vision.

The biased writer forms an opinion without all the facts, and then argues for this opinion by only referencing facts that support this false argument—actively and purposefully avoiding ideas that would cause trouble for their position. In this way bias is not merely "having an opinion," but having an opinion and refusing to change one's proposition regardless of whatever new evidence or ideas one may come across. It is a lazy and dangerous kind of thinking and writing.

The biased writer begins with a thesis in mind, and realized all too late that the thing is due the next morning, and must wrap it up. At this point it is simply easier to lie, dissemble, and avoid inconvenient sources to avoid having to rewrite one's whole argument.

The lazy instructor wants the biased writer to produce a thesis centered essay with 3 outside sources. The biased writer will follow their instructions and write the thesis statement first without thinking much about it. After all, the biased writer has been fine up until now, being driven about the streets with a crack whip and blinders on, pulling that cart and being fed carrots and barley and put away dry in their stall every evening.

The biased writer must now find 3 sources about their claim. What sources will they choose? If the writer wants to have some free time and get a good grade they'll do as they were told and disregard any inconvenient ideas that don't support their argument!

I think the main problem is that because we expect to hear the proposition, or the thesis, at the beginning of the essay—we also expect to write it first as well. But what's stopping an author from writing it last, and merely placing it in the introduction?

Most teachers of essay writing nowadays are happy enough to see that the writing student has merely included a thesis (proposition) in their writing, and gone some way to supporting that thesis with "facts." But what teacher has the time and patience to police against spurious logic, and silly arguments, or to make sure the student has considered the issue from all angles, and is prepared to meditate as they write?

Sometimes I wonder if it isn't baked into the culture—this resistance to showing any sign of weakness, to showing our work, and revealing our incomplete or partial thoughts and how we got our opinions in the first place: "Write a thesis", they say, "and defend it." But writing isn't combat! Why use words like "defend"? Are we under attack?

Instead of thinking of writing as building a fort to protect our precious ideas from invaders, why not instead think of our essays as boxes of sand, in which we can play and dream and have a good time? We make a proposal—construct a sand castle—and show it to the world! Who cares if someone knocks it down, if they replace it with something even cooler? Hey, maybe you even inspire them with your castle to make some improvements.

True essay writing requires humility, openness, and meditation—while bias and propaganda require just the opposite—severity, closedness, and an unwillingness to imagine another's perspective.

My proposition is this: write backwards. From the "bottom up" starting by reading and thinking, making lists, and being inspired by experience and life. Instead of beginning with the proposition and trying to prove it, try reversing the process, writing the thesis last, and start with the sources. That means, start by reading, and perhaps ask a question, or consider a hypothesis (an idea), trying this idea out, and doing more reading (research).

Once an original idea is in hand, it can be shown to the reader. Now the essay can be revised, and the proposition placed in the introduction. Voilà! An interesting, honest, and well supported essay!

Swift, Jonathan. "A Modest Proposal"

A Modest Proposal

For preventing the children of poor people in Ireland from being a burden on their parents or country, and for making them beneficial to the public.

Jonathan Swift

Edited by John Pfannkuchen

It is a sad sight for those who walk through this great town, or travel in the country, when they see the streets, the roads and front doors crowded with mothers, followed by three, four, or six children, all in rags, and begging for money. These mothers instead of being able to work for their honest livelihood are forced to spend all their time begging for their helpless infants who, as they grow up, either turn to stealing for lack of work, or leave their native country to fight for the Pretender in Spain, or sell themselves into slavery.

I think everyone agrees that this is a sad state of the kingdom, and therefore whoever can find a fair, cheap, and easy method of making these children useful citizens would deserve a statue of them erected as a savior of the nation.

But I intend to not only provide for the children of beggars. I have a solution that takes care of a whole number of infants at a certain age who are born to poor parents, like the ones that beg in the streets.

I have thought about this for many years, and considered the plans of others in our society. But I have always found these plans mistaken in their computation. It is true that a child just dropped from its mother may be supported by her milk for a solar year with little other nourishment: for no more than two shillings, which the mother could earn by begging. However, at one year old I propose to, instead of allowing them to be a burden upon their parents or the community or needing food and clothing for the rest of their lives, to instead allow the child to contribute to the feeding, and partly to the clothing, of many thousands.

Also there is another great advantage in my plan: it will prevent voluntary abortions, and the horrible practice of women murdering their bastard children. Too often mothers sacrifice poor innocent babies, more to avoid the expense than the shame, which would make the most savage and inhuman person feel pity.

There are about one and a half million people in this kingdom. Of these I calculate there may be about two hundred thousand couples whose wives are breeders. From this number I subtract thirty thousand couples, who are able to provide for their children, (although I don't think there are this many, given the state of things) but this being granted, there will remain one hundred and seventy thousand breeders. I again subtract fifty thousand, for those women who miscarry, or for the children who die by accident or disease within the first year. There remains only one hundred and twenty thousand children of poor parents born annually.

Therefore the question is: "How will these children be raised, and provided for?" Which I have already said is utterly impossible by all the methods already proposed, as things are now. Because we can neither employ these children in vocational work or agriculture; they can neither build houses, (I mean in the country) nor cultivate land: they can very rarely earn a living by stealing before the age of six. Although I admit they learn the basics much earlier; during which time they can be considered "thieves in training".

I am told by our merchants that a boy or a girl before twelve years old cannot be sold, and even when they come to this age, the merchant would not get more than three pounds, or three pounds and half a crown at most on the sale; which is not enough to account for even a quarter of the food and clothing needed to raise the child.

I shall now therefore humbly propose my own thoughts, which I hope will not be objected to.

I have been assured by a very knowing American of my acquaintance in London, that a young healthy child well nursed, is, at a year old, a most delicious nourishing and wholesome food, whether stewed, roasted, baked, or boiled; and I don't doubt that the child would be good in a fricassee, or a ragout.

I do therefore humbly offer it to public consideration, that of the hundred and twenty thousand children, that twenty thousand may be reserved for breed, whereas only twenty five percent should be males (which is more than we allow to sheep, black cattle, or swine). My reasoning is that these children are seldom born from marriage, therefore, one male will be sufficient to serve four females.

The remaining hundred thousand may, at a year old, be sold to high quality rich people through the kingdom, always advising the mother to let them suck plentifully in the final month to make them plump and fat for a good table. One child is enough for two dishes at a party with friends, and when the family dines alone, the fore or hind quarter will make a reasonable dish, and seasoned with a little pepper or salt will be very good boiled on the fourth day, especially in winter.

I have reckoned that on average a newborn weighing 12 pounds will, in a solar year, if well nursed, grow to 28 pounds.

I grant this food will be somewhat pricey, and therefore very proper for landlords, who, as they have already devoured most of the parents, seem to have the best claim to the children.

Infant's flesh will be in season throughout the year, but more plentiful in March, and a little before and after. We are told by a grave author, an eminent French physician, that fish being a popular diet, there are more children born in Roman Catholic countries about nine months after Lent. The markets will be more glutted than usual, because the number of Catholic infants, is at least three to one in this kingdom, and therefore it will have one other collateral advantage, by lessening the number of Catholics among us.

I have already computed the cost of nursing a beggar's child (which includes homesteaders, laborers, and eighty percent of the farmers) to be about two shillings per year, rags included. And I believe no bachelor would hesitate to pay ten shillings for the carcass of a good fat child, which would make four dishes of excellent nutritional meat, for when he has a friend or the whole family over for dinner. Therefor the young man will learn to be a good landlord, and grow popular among his tenants, and the mother will have eight shillings profit, and be fit for work till she has another child.

Those who are more thrifty (as I must confess the times require) may skin the carcass; the leather of which, when tanned, will make admirable gloves for ladies and summer boots for fine gentlemen.

As to our City of Dublin, shambles may be appointed for this purpose, in the most convenient parts of it, and there will be plenty of work for butchers; although I rather recommend buying the children alive, and dressing them hot from the knife, as we do roasting pigs.

A very worthy person, a true lover of his country, and whose virtues I highly esteem, offered a suggestion for my plan. He said that for many gentlemen of this kingdom, having lately hunted all their deer, that their loss of venison might be well replaced by the bodies of young lads and maidens, not exceeding fourteen years of age, nor under twelve. This is because there are so many children of this age, both male and female, about to starve for lack of work and jobs, and ready to be gotten rid of by their parents (if alive), or otherwise by their nearest relations. But with due respect to so excellent a friend, and so deserving a patriot, I cannot agree with him completely. Because, as for the males, my American acquaintance assured me from experience that their flesh is generally tough and lean, like that of our school-boys, because of continual exercise, and their taste disagreeable, and to fatten them would not make it any better. As for the females, it would be a loss to the public, because they would soon become breeders themselves: and besides, it's likely that some scrupulous people might be willing to say the practice, (although indeed very unjustly) borders on cruelty, which, I confess, has always been my strongest objection against any project, however well intended.

But in order to justify my friend, he confessed, that this idea was put into his head by the famous Salmanaazor, a native of the island Formosa, who had come to London over twenty years ago, and in conversation told my friend, that in his country, when any young person happened to be put to death, the executioner sold the carcass to quality people, as a kind of ; and that, in his time, the body of a plump girl of fifteen, who was crucified for an attempt to poison the Emperor, was sold to his imperial majesty's prime minister of state, and other great mandarins of the court in joints from the gibbet, at four hundred crowns. Neither indeed can I deny, that if the same use were made of several plump young girls in this town, who without one single penny to their names, cannot go abroad without a chair, and appear at a play-house and assemblies in foreign fineries which they never will pay for; the kingdom would not be the worse.

Some persons of a desponding spirit are in great concern about that vast number of poor people, who are old, diseased, or handicapped; and I have wondered what course may be taken, to ease the nation of so grievous an issue. But I am not in the least pain upon that matter, because it is very well known, that they are every day dying, and rotting, by cold and famine, and filth, and vermin, as fast as can be reasonably expected. And as to the young workers, they are now in almost as hopeful a condition. They cannot get work, and consequently pine away from lack of food, to a degree, that if at any time they are accidentally hired to common labor, they have not strength to perform it, and thus the country and themselves are happily delivered from the evils to come.

I have too long digressed, and therefore shall return to my subject. I think the advantages of my proposal are obvious and many, as well as of the highest importance.

For first, as I have already observed, it would greatly lessen the number of Catholics, with whom we are yearly over-run, being the principal breeders of the nation, as well as our most dangerous enemies, and who stay at home on purpose with a design to deliver the kingdom to the Pretender, hoping to take their advantage by the absence of so many good Protestants, who have chosen rather to leave their country, than stay at home and pay tithes against their conscience to an episcopal curate.

Secondly, The poorer tenants will have something valuable of their own, which by law may be made liable to a distress, and help to pay their landlord's rent, their corn and cattle being already seized, and money a thing unknown.

Thirdly, Whereas the maintenance of an hundred thousand children, from two years old, and upwards, cannot be computed at less than ten shillings a piece per annum, the nation's stock will be thereby increased fifty thousand pounds per annum, besides the profit of a new dish, introduced to the tables of all gentlemen of fortune in the kingdom, who have any refinement in taste. And the money will circulate among our selves, the goods being entirely of our own growth and manufacture.

Fourthly, The constant breeders, besides the gain of eight shillings sterling per annum by the sale of their children, will be rid of the charge of maintaining them after the first year.

Fifthly, This food would likewise bring great custom to taverns, where the vintners will certainly be so prudent as to procure the best receipts for dressing it to perfection; and consequently have their houses frequented by all the fine gentlemen, who justly value themselves upon their knowledge in good eating; and a skillful cook, who understands how to oblige his guests, will contrive to make it as expensive as they please.

Sixthly, This would be a great inducement to marriage, which all wise nations have either encouraged by rewards, or enforced by laws and penalties. It would increase the care and tenderness of mothers towards their children, when they were sure of a settlement for life to the poor babes, provided in some sort by the public, to their annual profit instead of expense. We should soon see an honest emulation among the married women, which of them could bring the fattest child to the market. Men would become as fond of their wives, during the time of their pregnancy, as they are now of their mares in foal, their cows in calf, or sow when they are ready to farrow; nor offer to beat or kick them (as is too frequent a practice) for fear of a miscarriage.

Many other advantages might be enumerated. For instance, the addition of some thousand carcasses in our exportation of barreled beef: the propagation of swine's flesh, and improvement in the art of making good bacon, so much wanted among us by the great destruction of pigs, too frequent at our tables; which are no way comparable in taste or magnificence to a well grown, fat yearly child, which roasted whole will make a considerable figure at a Lord Mayor's feast, or any other public entertainment. But this, and many others, I omit, being studious of brevity.

Supposing that one thousand families in this city, would be constant customers for infants flesh, besides others who might have it at merry meetings, particularly at weddings and christenings, I compute that Dublin would take off annually about twenty thousand carcasses; and the rest of the kingdom (where probably they will be sold somewhat cheaper) the remaining eighty thousand.

I can think of no one objection, that will possibly be raised against this proposal, unless it should be urged, that the number of people will be thereby much lessened in the kingdom. This I freely own, and 'twas indeed one principal design in offering it to the world. I desire the reader will observe, that I calculate my remedy for this one individual Kingdom of Ireland, and for no other that ever was, is, or, I think, ever can be upon Earth. Therefore let no man talk to me of other expedients: Of taxing our absentees at five shillings a pound: Of using neither clothes, nor household furniture, except what is of our own growth and manufacture: Of utterly rejecting the materials and instruments that promote foreign luxury: Of curing the expensiveness of pride, vanity, idleness, and gaming in our women: Of introducing a vein of parsimony, prudence and temperance: Of learning to love our country, wherein we differ even from Laplanders, and the inhabitants of Topinamboo: Of quitting our animosities and factions, nor acting any longer like the Jews, who were murdering one another at the very moment their city was taken: Of being a little cautious not to sell our country and consciences for nothing: Of teaching landlords to have at least one degree of mercy towards their tenants. Lastly, of putting a spirit of honesty, industry, and skill into our shop-keepers, who, if a resolution could now be taken to buy only our native goods, would immediately unite to cheat and exact upon us in the price, the measure, and the goodness, nor could ever yet be brought to make one fair proposal of just dealing, though often and earnestly invited to it.

Therefore I repeat, let no man talk to me of these and or similar ideas until he has at least some idea of how to put them into practice.

But, as to my self, having been wearied out for many years with offering vain, idle, visionary thoughts, and at length utterly despairing of success, I fortunately fell upon this proposal, which, as it is wholly new, so it has something solid and real, of no cost and little effort, that we can accomplish alone, and where there is no danger of harming England. For this kind of commodity cannot be exported, since flesh is too tender to transport in salt, although perhaps I could name a country which would be glad to eat up our whole nation without salt.

After all, I am not so close-minded that I would reject any offer proposed by wise men that is equally innocent, cheap, easy, and effective. But before I entertain other ideas I want the author or authors to consider two points. First, As things now stand, how will they find food and clothing for a hundred thousand useless mouths and backs? And secondly, There a million creatures in human figure throughout this kingdom, who cost the kingdom two million pounds sterling, adding those who are beggars by profession, to the bulk of farmers, homesteaders and laborers, with their wives and children, who are beggars in effect; I desire those politicians who dislike my ideas, and think they have a better idea, that they will first ask the parents of these mortals, whether they would not today want to have been sold for food at a year old, in the manner I suggest, and therefor having avoided all the misfortunes they have experienced, by the oppression of landlords, the impossibility of paying rent without money or work, the lack of common food, with neither house nor clothes to cover them from the weather, and the most inevitable prospect of inflicting the same or worse miseries upon their kind for ever?

I profess, in the sincerity of my heart, that I have no personal interest in trying to promoting this necessary work, having no other motive than the public good of my country, by advancing our trade, providing for infants, relieving the poor, and giving some pleasure to the rich. I have no children, by which I can propose to get a single penny; the youngest being nine years old, and my wife past child-bearing.

What is a Fact?

John Pfannkuchen

"…With a little practice you will see far better than those who quarrel about the shadows, whose knowledge is a dream only, whilst yours is a waking reality."

Plato

What is a fact? Most people I talk to seem to regard facts as little gods that they can carry around in their pockets and present at any opportune time, like say in argument, or to impress strangers. "Did you know…?" one starts off, "It's a fact that…" and on they drone, with authority.

Most people in our modern age have come to believe that facts are merely the truth, itemized. But sometimes, when I am being assaulted by a rather heavy torrent of facts, I begin to wonder if it's not so? I wonder if humans actually don't know the truth. So on this point I propose to discuss the difference between truth and fact.

A fact is what is known or proved to be true. Let's reflect on that for a moment. It's what's known to be or proven to be true. It's not true per say. Long story short, a fact is what people think is true at the time. What's a fact one minute could be old fashioned or backward thinking the next. If human knowledge is composed purely of facts, then, isn't it incomplete or simply wrong? I think so—but if that's the case, why do we build these sandcastles and cards of houses out of so many facts, just for the tide to come in and displace it all? I think facts are humanity's way of admitting we cannot possible know the truth, but settling for the next best thing anyways. To function human society needs something to rely on, some knowledge to base our decisions on—society is the act of cohabitation, or living together, and how difficult it would be to live with a bunch of people with which we disagree on everything!

And how do we establish facts, create them, manufacture, and publish them to the minds of men? I believe we can, ever since the Enlightenment, look toward science for the answers on scientific facts (what is demonstrated to always be true), but there are other kinds of facts as well, like historical facts (what we believe to have happened).

In these cases facts must be demonstrated—and not just once either—but in science the cause and effect that produced a fact must be easily reliably reproduced by different scientists. Consider the fact of gravity—and how it became a fact, and how humankind had gravity sewn up as "what goes up must come down" for so long, until a guy named Einstein came along and offered us his general theory of relativity.

"Well," you say, "what's the practical difference between truth and fact?" The practical difference between truth and fact is this: every day a fact is proven either partially or entirely wrong, and either changed, or entirely replaced by some newer, more correct fact. This is what we call "scientific progress."

Facts change. Facts are knowable. But the truth? The truth never changes. And we may never know it, and if we do know it, we can never know that we do know it. That's the implication of truth versus fact!

If an essayist understands that ultimate truth is beyond the grasp of human understanding—many possibilities are open to them—not least of which is the questioning of certain facts. Because—think of it! What a dull world we would live in if every child's imagination, and every artist's brush, and every writer's pen only held to known facts! What horrible science we would have—no science at all, really—if all people were satisfied with what they were told!

The essayist must question the facts of their society like grains of sand, pack them with water and make shapes of them, and wait for the tide to come and rearrange them once more, taking some out to sea, leaving others as a jumbled mess on the beach.

Allegory of the Cave

Plato

And now I will describe in a figure the enlightenment or unenlightenment of our nature:

Imagine human beings living in an underground den which is open towards the light; they have been there from childhood, having their necks and legs chained, and can only see into the den.

At a distance there is a fire, and between the fire and the prisoners a raised way, and a low wall is built along the way, like the screen over which marionette players show their puppets. Behind the wall appear moving figures, who hold in their hands various works of art, and among them images of men and animals, wood and stone, and some of the passers-by are talking and others silent.

"A strange parable, and strange captives."

They are ourselves, I replied; and they see only the shadows of the images which the fire throws on the wall of the den; to these they give names, and if we add an echo which returns from the wall, the voices of the passengers will seem to proceed from the shadows. Suppose now that you suddenly turn them round and make them look with pain and grief to themselves at the real images; will they believe them to be real?

Will not their eyes be dazzled, and will they not try to get away from the light to something which they are able to behold without blinking? And suppose further, that they are dragged up a steep and rugged ascent into the presence of the sun himself, will not their sight be darkened with the excess of light?

Some time will pass before they get the habit of perceiving at all; and at first they will be able to perceive only shadows and reflections in the water; then they will recognize the moon and the stars, and will at length behold the sun in his own proper place as he is.

Last of all they will conclude:--This is he who gives us the year and the seasons, and is the author of all that we see. How will they rejoice in passing from darkness to light! How worthless to them will seem the honors and glories of the den!

But now imagine further, that they descend into their old habitations;--in that underground dwelling they will not see as well as their fellows, and will not be able to compete with them in the measurement of the shadows on the wall; there will be many jokes about the man who went on a visit to the sun and lost his eyes, and if they find anybody trying to set free and enlighten one of their number, they will put him to death, if they can catch him.

Now the cave or den is the world of sight, the fire is the sun, the way upwards is the way to knowledge, and in the world of knowledge the idea of good is last seen and with difficulty, but when seen is inferred to be the author of good and right--parent of the lord of light in this world, and of truth and understanding in the other.

He who attains to the beatific vision is always going upwards; he is unwilling to descend into political assemblies and courts of law; for his eyes are apt to blink at the images or shadows of images which they behold in them--he cannot enter into the ideas of those who have never in their lives understood the relation of the shadow to the substance.

But blindness is of two kinds, and may be caused either by passing out of darkness into light or out of light into darkness, and a man of sense will distinguish between them, and will not laugh equally at both of them, but the blindness which arises from fullness of light he will deem blessed, and pity the other; or if he laugh at the puzzled soul looking at the sun, he will have more reason to laugh than the inhabitants of the den at those who descend from above.

There is a further lesson taught by this parable of ours. Some persons fancy that instruction is like giving eyes to the blind, but we say that the faculty of sight was always there, and that the soul only requires to be turned round towards the light. And this is conversion; other virtues are almost like bodily habits, and may be acquired in the same manner, but intelligence has a diviner life, and is indestructible, turning either to good or evil according to the direction given. Did you never observe how the mind of a clever rogue peers out of his eyes, and the more clearly he sees, the more evil he does? Now if you take someone like this, and cut away from him those leaden weights of pleasure and desire which bind his soul to earth, his intelligence will be turned round, and he will behold the truth as clearly as he now discerns his meaner ends.

And have we not decided that our rulers must neither be so uneducated as to have no fixed rule of life, nor so over-educated as to be unwilling to leave their paradise for the business of the world? We must choose out therefore the natures who are most likely to ascend to the light and knowledge of the good; but we must not allow them to remain in the region of light; they must be forced down again among the captives in the den to partake of their labors and honors.

"Will they not think this a hardship?"

You should remember that our purpose in framing the State was not that our citizens should do what they like, but that they should serve the State for the common good of all. May we not fairly say to our philosopher,--Friend, we do you no wrong; for in other States philosophy grows wild, and a wild plant owes nothing to the gardener, but you have been trained by us to be the rulers and kings of our hive, and therefore we must insist on your descending into the den. You must, each of you, take your turn, and become able to use your eyes in the dark, and with a little practice you will see far better than those who quarrel about the shadows, whose knowledge is a dream only, whilst yours is a waking reality.

It may be that the saint or philosopher who is best fitted, may also be the least inclined to rule, but necessity is laid upon him, and he must no longer live in the heaven of ideas.

And this will be the salvation of the State. For those who rule must not be those who are desirous to rule; and, if you can offer to our citizens a better life than that of rulers generally is, there will be a chance that the rich, not only in this world's goods, but in virtue and wisdom, may bear rule. And the only life which is better than the life of political ambition is that of philosophy, which is also the best preparation for the government of a State.

On Readers

John Pfannkuchen

I try to imagine who the reader—a person, I presume, or perhaps a very learned pet, that has gotten hold of its master's bookshelf. But what is the character of the entity, whether it be animal, vegetable, mineral, or other? As an essayist, I put pen to paper, and wonder "Who will read this? A passing stranger? A close relation?"

I can imagine and guess, and build magnificent profiles of the people for whom these essays have been penned—but that's not the exercise of this essay, nor is it the point. I will admit that it is probably impossible to say with certainty for whom an essay was written, unless named directly by the author. Even then it might be a lie.

But it's my proposition that, for every good essay, that there was a someone out there somewhere for whom it was written specifically. Not just "people in general," or a "certain kind of person." No—there must have been an image of the person for whom it was written burned into the essay.

It seems that in some essays the writer is very passionate about their subject, and in others the writer seems to only follow some minute and fleeting strand of logic, like a child running through the forest. In some essays the writing is familiar and comfortable, focused and clean; in others it is meandering, unsure of itself, and widely varied in scope. It is because of some reader, the knowledge of this reader, that the essayist can know exactly how to write—because of the anticipation of this reader, a thousand questions have been answered without needing to be asked! Questions on style, substance, focus, language, scope, language, and more.

When one writes for a reader the fact cannot be escaped. It may be a close relation, known for years, like a sibling, a parent, or a lover, or a childhood friend, or a passing acquaintance, someone met at a party or a cafe once, and with whom was shared a very engaging argument, or a stranger on the street that was stood in line with to buy lunch—or the vendor himself. The writer cannot help but to be haunted by the person and situation for whom the writing applies, to imagine certain qualities of their character. The writing could even be for someone whom the essayist has never personally met, someone the news—the President of the United States, a Syrian refugee, a man who rescued puppies from a burning pet store, a woman who puts chocolate syrup on hot dogs. But why?

I have decided that it's important to bear someone in mind, to write for someone, when penning an essay. Here is why:

1. The essay becomes more particular than general—by choosing a person to write for, the essayist should also choose a reason for writing for this person. This reason has bound up in it the essayist's memory of the person. This memory, and reason for the essayist's memory, lends itself to a topic.

2. The essay becomes more interesting to the essayist—by choosing something that has resided in memory, the essayist can count on there being some emotional connection to that memory, because after all there is likely a reason they remembered it, even if they're unsure of what that reason is. The essayist will discover, by layers, and stages, and through very careful and delicate investigation, why this memory has stayed with them.

3. The essayist knows how to write "for" that person—many writers struggle with the question of what level of language is appropriate to use for their essays. They fuss over first person, second person, or third person. They worry about contractions like "isn't, wasn't, and aren't." But when one writes for someone they need only draw on their impression of that person, and their purpose for writing for them, to guide them in these decisions.

4. The essay has a purpose, instead of being purposeless.

6. The essay has a build in audience! The beauty of writing for

a particular person is that there are likely 100,000 people like that person, and in that case at least a billion people who either know or have heard of someone similar to the person that is being written for. In other words, when one writes for only one particular person the opposite thing happens: their work becomes more relatable!

In this list of benefits we find some guidelines as well, for whom we shouldn't write for. Many a first year essayist will take the lazy route and try to write "for their instructor." This can and could work, unless of course one feels absolutely no passion regarding their instructor. If one has no specific memories on which to draw, if an essayist has no disagreement, or message to convey, or encouragement to offer—if indeed the essayist has no memory whatsoever that sticks in their mind—then writing for their instructor should not be a first choice.

The essayist must think of someone for whom they can write for. Someone who has left a lasting impression on them, if only in passing. It is this impression the essayist draws on.

But! You cry, it is very well and good to write for a particular person—but what if I want my writing to be readable by a general audience? Well then, I reply, look again at the essays I referenced earlier, and ask yourself if these are passable, if you can or cannot relate to them, if you have learned nothing valuable from them, or if you did not enjoy the time you spent reading them?

It is true; in the end an essayist may need to change their work in small degrees to meet certain requirements—for publication, or merely for a writing instructor—but that is a question of process. I believe it is best to begin with someone particular in mind, and if other people must be taken into consideration, let them guide the editing long after the first draft is complete, and only if it is absolutely necessary.

The Literary Uses of Experience

Elisabeth Morris

"Did you enjoy it very much?" asked a lady of a little girl whom she met coming away from an entertainment. "Yes," answered the child, but there was a note of reservation in her voice. Then she threw back her head half defiantly and added, "But don't you think it's hard that I can never go to anything with out having to go home and write an account of it afterwards?" Hard, indeed! And yet harder that the tyrant who imposed the requirement happened to be the child's mother—one of those over trained and overanxious people who continue to bring the higher education of women into disrepute. Of course, our sympathies are all with the little girl. We recognize that her protest was a sign, not of naughtiness, but of health. There was some thing wrong about this continual exploiting of immediate experience, and she knew it and rebelled against it. The little incident has lain in my mind for years, serving as a nucleus round which ruminating thoughts have gathered regarding the whole subject of the literary uses of experience.

The writer of fiction, if he is at once sensitive and conscientious, must often find himself in a dilemma. He is urged to "write out of his own experience," since otherwise his work will not ring true. Look at Jane Austen, he is told, sitting quiet and feminine under her lamp and writing her tales of the little every day doings of little everyday folk! Behold her, even refusing to undertake the great historical romance urged upon her by Royalty itself, because it "fell outside her experience." Here is a model for all young writers. Very well. The obedient artist turns him to the Me about him, and, sure enough, there is indeed plenty of material. Here is an aunt who, considered as a "character," is ripe to be picked and set in a book. Here is a sister-in-law, whose experiences with her servants, literally set down, would make a most readable and instructive set of papers for some woman's journal. Or, in sterner vein, here is a brother or a friend whose business experience or whose love-affair offers a tempting subject. Finally, the writer realizes that in his own life he has only to put forth his hand and take what he needs. Yes, for once the general voice is speaking the truth: his material does, indeed, lie close about him.

Suppose, then, he takes it, uses it. We know very well what happens: "Have you read that last thing by young Bellerophon? The one about the Lady and the Cook? Of course we all know who it is he means she simply can't keep a cook—it's the scandal of the street, the number she has in a month. But I don't think that gives him any right—you know what I mean?" If it is his own experience he has used, the results are different, but no better: "You saw that story of his? Yes—it is interesting. I suppose you knew it was his own experience yes,—he went all through that a few years ago—oh, he's all right now, but his family felt terribly at the time, and I couldn't help wondering how they d like to see it all—sort of spread out in print this way."

Has it then always been so? Did Euripides's contemporaries look askance at him because, under the thin disguise of Clytemnestra, he had written up a sister-in-law? Did those who listened to Sappho's lyrics shudder a little and murmur, "Beautiful, of course, but—how could she?" Did Horace's acquaintance raise their eyebrows over some of the personalities in the odes? And did Catullus's pretty little lady wish he had not coined her and her pet bird into verse? We cannot tell. Time has wiped out the original material, whatever it was, and left only the artistic rendering.

About our contemporaries, however, one hears persistent rumors: here is one composing a poem on his son's death even before the burial, and handing it to a friend for possible publication. Here is another using the love-affairs of his friends—quite recognizably—to make his plots. Here is another setting one of our centers of social service aflame with indignation because she had, in their opinion, written them up. Here is a New England town boiling over with resentment because one to whom they had shown hospitality had rewarded them by "putting them into a book." I saw recently a newspaper notice of a suit brought by a man against his wife be cause, as he alleged, her latest novel made use of their life together in such a way as to reflect unpleasantly on his character.

Whether in these and other cases the complainants are justified, it is neither possible nor necessary to consider. The moral question involved in the use of real life is so complex that each instance would have to be handled separately. It was once, they say, decided that a man might sniff the odors of another man's dinner without having to pay for it, but whether he may bottle the aroma of another man's life while it is yet hot, for the purpose of serving it again, perhaps cold or luke-warm, to the general public, is quite an other matter. It is at least clear that the use of experience may be fraught with perplexity for the writer. There is a curiously frank acknowledgment of this in a short story by Mrs. Wharton, called "Copy." It represents two authors, a man and a woman, who had once been in love with each other, meeting after the lapse of years. Each has the other's old love-letters, and each suddenly realizes what wonderful "copy" these would make. There is much skill-ful and intricate fencing between them, but at last, moved by a scarce-ly acknowledged reverence for the past, by some obscure impulse of loyalty to it, they burn all the letters. The story may serve as a reminder that, whereas we are apt to know the cases where writers have yielded to temptation,—if temptation it be,—we do not know the cases where they have resisted.

But such recognition by authors themselves of the moral prob-lems involved seems to be rather rare. In general, though readers may question or condemn, the writer himself is likely to be unconscious of offense. I met an instance of this once when I was thrown for a short time with a writer of stories. She had told me a good deal about her life at a certain period several years before, and among other matters had mentioned a teapot of delicate workmanship, and how it happened to get broken. Later, reading her newest book, I came upon the incident of the teapot. As I went on, I noticed other correspondences with what I knew to be fact. I was interested, and one day I brought the thing up.

"It gives a good deal of your life in Rouen that winter, doesn't it?" I said, innocent of offense. Instantly her color flamed and her eyes showed deep annoyance. She took me up quickly: "It has nothing whatever to do with my life there. How could you have supposed that?" Naturally, I dropped the matter, but, that being my first close encounter with the artistic temperament, I was very much puzzled. There was no doubting her sincerity, but there was also no doubting the fact that her life of that winter had got into her book.

Again, a young girl, just out of college, wrote her first novel. Her college friends read it with consternation. "But," they exclaimed, "this is Anna herself! This is Anna's step-mother! This is just what did happen that time when her father died! This is not a novel, it is a diary! Anna is going too far." But two years later Anna wrote another novel, containing more shocks for her friends. Here, they claimed, was Anna's engagement and marriage. Here was Anna's husband. Here were her experiences at the birth of her child. They approached her about it. What satisfaction did they get? Just as little as I got in the teapot incident. Anna absolutely denied any connection between her novel and her own life, and Anna was truth itself. At the same time, Anna, speaking as an artist, ex cathedra, said firmly, that if anything in her life should be needed for the artistic completeness of her literary work, she would not hesitate to use it, art being in a realm so much higher than one's personal feelings.

From all this, it is obvious enough that something happens to the artist, while he is artist, which imposes on him standards different from ours—different even from his own when he is not in the artistic mood. So that although as ordinary man in ordinary intercourse he may, for example, be a most reserved person, who would find it easier to cut out his own heart and slice it up for his friends than to cull out bits of his deepest life and serve them up in conversation, yet on the printed page we may find him doing something very much like this exploiting in luminous paragraphs moods and feelings which to most of us seem too deep-lying to be touched upon, save by allusive implication, even with our most beloved friends. I have read articles in the magazines that made me uncomfortable, not because they were shocking on the few lines along which one is conventionally supposed to be shocked, but because they seemed to me to involve such crude exposure of the soul as nothing but hysteria could excuse. A friend of mine, trying to read a certain essay—if one may apply the term to a ten-page prose lyric expressing the author's personal mood—suddenly threw it down, exclaiming, "This is too painful—it's raw! It's bleeding!" At first glance, one is inclined to put such writers in the class with a certain little girl I knew, who climbed up into her mother's lap and said, with more than a suggestion of gloating anticipation, "Now, mother, let's talk about my faults!" But is it perhaps we who are wrong? Is our vaunted New Eng land reserve, after all, at fault? Are these writers showing us the way, and is there in the future to be no reserve in life as there is, apparently, for them, none in art? Or are we trying to reconcile two different worlds when we allow ourselves to be troubled by the artist's intimacy of revelation? Are we shrinking from the spiritual nude in art as some people still shrink from the physical nude, merely because our artistic perceptions have been incompletely developed? These are questions which I am better prepared to ask than to answer, yet a sidelight on them has seemed to come through my meditations on memory. For years it has beset me, this thought of the magic possessed by memory. Where it touches it transforms. Nearly everybody's memory is artistic, or at any rate more nearly artistic than his immediate perceptions. Children are following a true instinct when they beg for a story "about something you remember, that happened a long time ago," for the things that we thus remember have a way of gathering into themselves any flavor of poetic feeling that may be in our nature. What is it, then, that memory does?

For one thing, it selects. In our immediate perceptions we often cannot see the woods for the trees. Memory knows no such trouble. Its trees are often blurred, but its woods stretch far and blue, dark-shadowed and full of meanings. For another, it distances. Through it we escape from the importunity of practical issues. Memory knows no practical issues; things are clear but we cannot alter them, they are real but we can neither seize nor avoid them. The light of memory is a light that never was on sea or land—mellow and soft, full of tender interpretations, of delicate emphases, of exquisite withdrawals.

If memory, then, is a kind of art, art is a kind of memory. Like memory it selects, like memory it interprets. It, too, has its emphases and its withdrawals, and like memory it creates its own remoteness. For to see beauty, or, more broadly, to see the world with our perceptions alert to its aesthetic significance, we must withdraw from it, we must hold it away from us. While we are seeing the beauty of the lion who crouches in the jungle grass, we do, in that instant of perception, ignore the necessity for killing him, the danger of his killing us. Wandering in a white sea-fog over the marshes, we may, in a realization of its weird loveliness, entirely lose our sense of the menace it holds for us. These things take upon themselves, for the moment, something of the quality of memories. Was it, as Gilbert Murray suggests, an acknowledgment of this kinship between memory and art, that the Greeks wove into the fiber of their philosophic myth, when they made Memory the mother of the Muses?

But the relation is one of kinship only, not of identity. For whereas the remoteness of memory is unalterable and eternal, the remoteness of our art-perceptions is apt to be momentary, and in part at least a matter of our own choice. While memory gently but insistently urges us into something much like the aesthetic attitude toward the treasures it offers us, real life, with its lions, and its fog, makes a more complex appeal. There is only one way to take memory, but there are two ways of taking life, the aesthetic and the practical. Between these two there is a plenteous lack of understanding. "What right," says the practical man, "have you to stand around just looking at lions and fog, when there is so much that is really important to be done about them?" He views everything in one of two aspects: it is either a thing that he can do something to, or it is a thing that can do something to him. He thinks of things, not as they are, but with reference to what he would like to do with them or to them. Perception for its own sake, expression for its own sake, makes no appeal to him. Even memory he forces into practical service, and allows its other powers to atrophy.

At the other extreme is the aesthete, who lives to taste the flavors of his perceptions and to express them. "Lions and fog are so wonderful," he cries, "Look at them! Only look!" And while the practical man calls him a dreamer and a trifler and a shirk, he calls the practical man a barbarian and a prude, who is afraid to look at life as it really is. He undergoes experience as all men must, but almost in the moment of its occurrence it be comes something apart from him, delicately valued in the withdrawal of the aesthetic mood. Thus life for him is continually under going such a transmutation as for most of us only the magic of memory can bring about. While he is yet white with indignation, he may say to himself, "This is anger." While he loves, he realizes, "This is indeed passion." Probably the two moods, of emotion and appreciation, are not really simultaneous, they may alternate with lightning-like interplay. But they seem to the observer, and even, perhaps, to the possessor, like two streams flowing on together, like two runners racing abreast, one oblivious of all but the mad motion, the other with eyes, not on the goal, not blind with the rush of it, but turned, deeply observant, on the face of his companion.

It is, then, this capacity for immediate aloofness from experience, this power of withdrawal into a realm closely resembling that of memory, which makes possible for the artist some of the things that shock us. But though it may to some extent explain his state of mind, it does not perhaps make us approve of it any more heartily. For there is something repellent to us in the ability thus to distance experience, either one's own or another's. It seems not quite warmly human. When memory, through its distancing power, gradually and gently loosens the bonds of reserve, we permit it, we even love it, because it is a universal experience. But when the aesthetic mood loosens these bonds, not gradually but at once, by merely, as it were, taking a step to one side, we shrink a little. An old man, we feel, may say things of his youth that his youth could not have said of itself even if it had known them.

What we probably do not realize is that people differ enormously in their rate of re action to life. An experience which in one person may after its occurrence not come to full fruition in consciousness for months or years, may in another pass through the same phases in a few hours or even minutes. Yet the lower rate is so much commoner that there is a presumption against the immediate coining of experience into artistic expression. If, after a great bereavement, a man sits down at once and embodies it in a poem, if, when an overwhelming passion has barely burned itself out, he proceeds to set it forth in a novel, we find ourselves suspecting, even before we examine the case, that either the bereavement and the passion will prove to have been not so overwhelming after all, or else that their artistic rendering will prove not really artistic.

This last point is one which needs some attention. So far I have been considering the use of experience chiefly in its ethical aspects. It is clear that the use of other people as material for art often exposes writers to sharp and persistent criticism. I have suggested that there are reasons grounded in the processes of the artistic temperament, why this criticism is often not in the least understood by the writers themselves. But, aside from this question of the moral right of an artist to make use of another's life, there is a second question, namely, what is the effect of the immediate use of experience on the art-product itself? Morals aside, does it tend to pro duce good art? In the case of one's own life, for instance, where it may be argued that one has the moral right to use whatever one likes, it might be of interest to inquire whether, purely from the effect on the art-product, it is not often a mistake to hurry forward into expression. The continual tasting and labeling of sensation tends to make sensation itself a little thin, or at least not quite true. And it is conceivable that lions and fog can never be completely grasped, even aesthetically, save by one who has first, in complete abandonment to practical needs, fought the lions and groped through the fog. Experience, entered upon with a conscious aesthetic purpose, may be thus deprived of its last, keenest quality, and even when not thus taken, it may, if too hastily garnered into expression, never reach, even as pure expression, the mellowness of maturity that might otherwise have been attained.

The pressure upon the artist urging him to serve green fruit instead of waiting for it to ripen, has, of course, never been so great as now. But there is, I believe, pressure of another sort, far stronger and far more respect able, arising naturally and inevitably out of our present habits of thought. With the enormous growth of scientific interest—interest in facts, and faith in what they may lead us to—we have developed a reverence for accuracy, patience, thoroughness, and discrimination. "Study your own thumb-nail enough," Agassiz used to say, "and you will find enough to occupy you for a lifetime." And he was fond of testing young students by giving them a cross-section of a broom-handle and seeing what they made of it. This was excellent. Applied to coral islands and earth worms and infusoria and sea-urchins, it is producing stupendous results. And now attention is being turned inward upon the human spirit itself—not, indeed, for the first time, but for the first time with just these methods. Man himself, as Walter Bagehot pointed out a generation ago, has become an antiquity—that is, a subject for scientific investigation. And the artist as well as the scientist has caught the habit of thumb-nail study and inspection of broom-handle sections. This too is excellent. It is compelling writers to an honesty of aim, a meticulous precision in technique, of a kind that has never been equaled. The scientist who would sit in his study and write about the processes of nature "out of his head" is now in disrepute. Similarly, the journalist who would write about the poor without first having "done the slums" would be very much behind the times. We may swing back again to a love for the fantastic and fanciful, but at present we are lost in admiration of the obviously truthful.

These things go by waves. For there is always a tendency, when we have become impressed with the excellence of some quality, to see that quality everywhere, to the exclusion of all others. If we love blue, we see blue in everything. If we have been deeply moved by the excellence of courage, or of honesty, or of kindness, we translate all the moral virtues into terms of sincerity or honesty or kindness. There are reasons, in the underlying unity of the world, why this can rather easily be done, both with colors and with moral qualities, but it has to be done carefully.

So with theories of art. Sometimes it is attempted to state all the aesthetic virtues in terms of morality. Ruskin did this very appealingly but not quite satisfyingly. Often they have been stated in terms of beauty, and this also has its pitfalls. Just now, in the flush of our enthusiasm for the ideals which science seems to have set up, we are stating them in terms of sincerity. This disposes of certain problems, for instance, the problem of ugliness; but it leads to other difficulties. For even in the scientific observation of fact there is such a thing as losing the significance of detail through absorption in its immediate aspects, and this is yet more easily possible in the realm of art. There may have been a time when artists needed to be called sharply to account for the sincerity of their intention and the accuracy of their work, but at present they are much more apt to offer us these in place of something else that would be of still greater value. We are all of us in danger of falling into two fallacies: first, of assuming that accuracy of detail in the art-product is the most necessary condition of its high quality as art, and second—granting that such accuracy is very desirable—the fallacy of assuming that it will necessarily be attained in the highest degree through sincere study and immediately faithful rendering of detail. If our theory makes these two assumptions, it becomes very difficult to explain why a monument of honest and masterly self-analysis like Amiel's "Journal" is not, as a work of art, greater than "Hamlet." The truth of art has never, perhaps, been successfully defined; but we must see, when we really face the question, that it is something different from sincerity in the artist or accuracy in his product. For we have to cover the truth of Shakespeare with half his detail wrong, the truth of Conrad, with all his detail right, the truth of Euripides, with whose detail we have now simply nothing to do, the truth of Rodin, who never works from a single pose but expresses an understanding born of fused impressions. It must be clear that this truth can never be expressed, either objectively in terms of accuracy, or subjectively in terms of sincerity, except by wrenching these terms away from all their usual connotations. It must rather be conceived as a kind of vision that requires, indeed, an atmosphere of sincerity and is fed by experience—any experience, it hardly matters what,—but which requires also a certain remoteness and detachment of spirit. I sometimes wonder whether we should not be gainers if our writers, like the Greeks, did a life-work first—a good chunk of hard, practically serviceable living—as farmers or manufacturers or administrators or teachers, and only after this were permitted to fall upon their task as artists. De Morgan and Conrad among the moderns are shining examples of the possibilities of this program; and with them we might class the literary men who have most of their lives swung a definite business, carrying on their artistic labors, as it were, "with their left hand"—Matthew Arnold and Lamb, for example. It is, indeed, only rather recently that writing has become lucrative enough to permit of its being chosen early as a profession.

Probably we should lose something. Doubtless we should gain something. Doubtless we should be spared much of the hasty mongering of experience to which I have been referring. In thinking of this, one is tempted to use the neat phrase of that prince of dreamers who was also in his lighter moments the prince of teases: "You cannot, sir, take from me anything that I will more willingly part withal."

On Introductions

John Pfannkuchen

Personally, I hate introductions. I do not know why. I avoid the moment—with all its falsity and pomp. I never shake hands, except when playing with dogs, and making introductions. I also find looking people in the eyes, smiling, and pretending that I didn't wish to be on a couch somewhere somewhat dishonest. Sometimes I have the opportunity to meet someone very interesting, but in these cases an introduction is altogether forgotten in place of some interesting circumstance or conversation that seems to have arisen between myself and the stranger, like the spark of a wildfire. Eventually will may get to exchanging names, but the anxiety is mostly gone; replaced by a tacit and felt interest in whatever caused us to converse in the first place—and perhaps a shared interest in the other person. In this way chance encounters are the bread and butter of a happy life, while the sideshow of being introduced to a mutual acquaintance—someone we have no choice in meeting, and no previous interest, is a kind of necessary evil.

I harbor the suspicion, the theory, that introductions in writing can be just as pleasant and interesting and invigorating as chance encounters with interesting, like minded people—or they can go the opposite way as well. But introductions in writing aren't by chance from the writer's perspective. The essayist has set out to introduce something, and it's a chance as to whether or not an interested party will pick it up and read it.

Now we must ask ourselves this question: what is the point of an introduction? Why not just throw something down and call it a day? Let the reader figure out which way is up, and which way down?

The typical answer is because when we take the time to consider the reader, we have to admit that it might be terribly confusing to have no introduction whatsoever—or would it? If I were to merely launch into a heady discussion of material science with an eight year girl in the jelly bean store, would I be well received, by her or her legal guardians, much less the store clerks? In this case, I'm not sure an introduction could save me—I have chosen the wrong audience for my thoughts.

But if I were standing before a microprocessor fabrication plant, with a class of fellow physicists, would an introduction be necessary? Some of my fellows might get the idea that, since we are equals, and they already are familiar with the facts, that I am talking down to them, and wasting their time. But for politeness sake they would be obligated to stand and nod, and wait to be let out for recess.

But let's say that the reader and I have something in common, and we are on the verge of discovering this something at the same time. That feels more like a chance encounter—an insight shared by two people.

In this case, let me make a proposition, that the whole point, then, of an introduction, is to get the reader from the title to the main content of your essay. If your introduction doesn't add something, then it shouldn't exist; it's redundant, and all things redundant have no business being printed to dead trees, and passed on to unwitting readers.

So what purpose could an introduction possibly have, there sandwiched between the Title and the Body of your essay?

The one idea that often gets lost in most discussions of essay writing is how fun an instruction could, should, and ought to be. Most people open up with a bland, if not downright eye-wateringly boring segue from the most general to their essay topic. Some examples of bad writing include:

1. Defining a Word or Concept (that the reader already understands).

2. Introducing the Topic (that the reader should already be familiar with).

3. Anything that starts with or contains the words: "Throughout

History…"

4. Silly rhetorical questions: "Have you ever wondered…?"

Many writers make the mistake of thinking they must being their essays with a general, or vague introduction. One of the reasons this happens are because the writer doesn't know a few things. They don't know:

1. Who they're writing for (Reader).

2. What they're writing for (Purpose).

So their introduction can't possibly be anything but general, since it's an introduction for literally everyone and for every possible purpose. It's a natural thing to speak in general, and to use dictionary definitions to fluff up such an introduction. But this makes for horribly bad writing—because it does the opposite of what an introduction is supposed to do, which is get the reader from the Title to the Body of your essay. A poorly written, vague, bland, and boring introduction will stop the reader in their tracks, and have them reaching for some other writer who knows who they're writing for and why.

On Getting Respected in Inns and Hotels

Hilaire Belloc

To begin at the beginning is, next to ending at the end, the whole art of writing; as for the middle you may fill it in with any rubble that you choose. But the beginning and the end, like the strong stone outer walls of medieval buildings, contain and define the whole.

And there is more than this: since writing is a human and a living art, the beginning being the motive and the end the object of the work, each inspires it; each runs through organically, and the two between them give life to what you do.

So I will begin at the beginning and I will lay down this first principle, that religion and the full meaning of things has nowhere more disappeared from the modern world than in the department of Guide Books.

For a Guide Book will tell you always what are the principal and most vulgar sights of a town; what mountains are most difficult to climb, and, invariably, the exact distances between one place and another. But these things do not serve the End of Man. The end of man is Happiness, and how much happier are you with such a knowledge? Now there are some Guide Books which do make little excursions now and then into the important things, which tell you (for instance) what kind of cooking you will find in what places, what kind of wine in countries where this beverage is publicly known, and even a few, more daring than the rest, will give a hint or two upon hiring mules, and upon the way that a bargain should be conducted, or how to fight.

But with all this even the best of them do not go to the moral heart of the matter. They do not give you a hint or an idea of that which is surely the basis of all happiness in travel. I mean, the art of gaining respect in the places where you stay. Unless that respect is paid you, you are more miserable by far than if you had stayed at home, and I would ask anyone who reads this whether he can remember one single journey of his which was not marred by the evident contempt which the servants and the owners of taverns showed for him wherever he went?

It is therefore of the first importance, much more important than any question of price or distance, to know something of this art; it is not difficult to learn, moreover it is so little exploited that if you will but learn it you will have a sense of privilege and of upstanding among your fellows worth all the holidays which were ever taken in the world.

Of this Respect which we seek, out of so many human pleasures, a facile, and a very false interpretation is that it is the privilege of the rich, and I even knew one poor fellow who forged a check and went to gaol [jail] in his desire to impress the host of the "Spotted Dog," near Barnard Castle. It was an error in him, as it is in all who so imagine. The rich in their degree fall under this contempt as heavily as any, and there is no wealth that can purchase the true awe which it should be your aim to receive from waiters, serving-wenches, boot-blacks, and publicans.

I knew a man once who set out walking from Oxford to Stow-in-the-Wold, from Stow-in-the-Wold to Cheltenham, from Cheltenham to Ledbury, from Ledbury to Hereford, from Hereford to New Rhayader (where the Cobbler lives), and from New Rhayader to the end of the world which lies a little west and north of that place, and all the way he slept rough under hedges and in stacks, or by day in open fields, so terrified was he at the thought of the contempt that awaited him should he pay for a bed. And I knew another man who walked from York to Thirsk, and from Thirsk to Darlington, and from Darlington to Durham, and so on up to the border and over it, and all the way he pretended to be extremely poor so that he might be certain the contempt he received was due to nothing of his own, but to his clothes only: but this was an indifferent way of escaping, for it got him into many fights with miners, and he was arrested by the police in Lanchester; and at Jedburgh, where his money did really fail him, he had to walk all through the night, finding that no one would take in such a tatterdemalion. The thing could be done much more cheaply than that, and much more respectably, and you can acquire with but little practice one of many ways of achieving the full respect of the whole house, even of that proud woman who sits behind glass in front of an enormous ledger; and the first way is this:—

As you come into the place go straight for the smoking-room, and begin talking of the local sport: and do not talk humbly and tentatively as so many do, but in a loud authoritative tone. You shall insist and lay down the law and fly into a passion if you are contradicted. There is here an objection which will arise in the mind of every niggler and boggler who has in the past very properly been covered with ridicule and become the butt of the waiters and stable-yard, which is, that if one is ignorant of the local sport, there is an end to the business. The objection is ridiculous. Do you suppose that the people whom you hear talking around you are more learned than yourself in the matter? And if they are do you suppose that they are acquainted with your ignorance? Remember that most of them have read far less than you, and that you can draw upon an experience of travel of which they can know nothing; do but make the plunge, practicing first in the villages of the Midlands, I will warrant you that in a very little while bold assertion of this kind will carry you through any tap-room or bar-parlour in Britain.

I remember once in the holy and secluded village of Washington under the Downs, there came in upon us as we sat in the inn there a man whom I recognized though he did not know me—for a journalist—incapable of understanding the driving of a cow, let alone horses: a prophet, a socialist, a man who knew the trend of things and so forth: a man who had never been outside a town except upon a motor bicycle, upon which snorting beast indeed had he come to this inn. But if he was less than us in so many things he was greater than us in this art of gaining respect in Inns and Hotels. For he sat down, and when they had barely had time to say good day to him he gave us in minutest detail a great run after a fox, a run that never took place. We were fifteen men in the room; none of us were anything like rich enough to hunt, and the lie went through them like an express. This fellow "found" (whatever that may mean) at Gumber Corner, ran right through the combe (which, by the way, is one of those bits of land which have been stolen bodily from the English people), cut down the Sutton Road, across the railway at Coates (and there he showed the cloven hoof, for your liar always takes his hounds across the railway), then all over Egdean, and killed in a field near Wisborough. All this he told, and there was not even a man there to ask him whether all those little dogs and horses swam the Rother or jumped it. He was treated like a god; they tried to make him stop but he would not. He was off to Worthing, where I have no doubt he told some further lies upon the growing of tomatoes under glass, which is the main sport of that district. Similarly, I have no doubt, such a man would talk about boats at King's Lynn, murder with violence at Croydon, duck shooting at Ely, and racing anywhere.

Then also if you are in any doubt as to what they want of you, you can always change the scene. Thus fishing is dangerous for even the poor can fish, and the chances are you do not know the names of the animals, and you may be putting salt-water fish into the stream of Lambourne, or talking of salmon upon the Upper Thames. But what is to prevent you putting on a look of distance and marvel, and conjuring up the North Atlantic for them? Hold them with the cold and the fog of the Newfoundland seas, and terrify their simple minds with whales.

A second way to attain respect, if you are by nature a silent man, and one which I think is always successful, is to write before you go to bed and leave upon the table a great number of envelopes which you should address to members of the Cabinet, and Jewish money-lenders, dukes, and in general any of the great. It is but slight labor, and for the contents you cannot do better than put into each envelope one of those advertisements which you will find lying about. Then next morning you should gather them up and ask where the post is: but you need not post them, and you need not fear for your bill. Your bill will stand much the same, and your reputation will swell like a sponge.

And a third way is to go to the telephone, since there are telephones nowadays, and ring up whoever in the neighborhood is of the greatest importance. There is no law against it, and when you have the number you have but to ask the servant at the other end whether it is not somebody else's house. But in the meanwhile your night in the place is secure.

And a fourth way is to tell them to call you extremely early, and then to get up extremely late. Now why this should have the effect it has I confess I cannot tell. I lay down the rule empirically and from long observation, but I may suggest that perhaps it is the combination of the energy you show in early rising, and of the luxury you show in late rising: for energy and luxury are the two qualities which menials most admire in that governing class to which you flatter yourself you belong. Moreover the strength of will with which you sweep aside their inconvenience, ordering one thing and doing another, is not without its effect, and the stir you have created is of use to you.

And the fifth way is to be Strong, to Dominate and to Lead. To be one of the Makers of this world, one of the Builders. To have the more Powerful Will. To arouse in all around you by mere Force of Personality a feeling that they must Obey. But I do not know how this is done.

Conclusions

John Pfannkuchen

As I finish reading the essay Hilaire Belloc's "On Getting Respected in Inns and Hotels," I find myself wondering: where is the conclusion? Where does it begin? Then I wonder, how did it make me feel? If I search my feelings, maybe that will be a clue as to where the essayist begins concluding. Perhaps it's at the beginning of the final paragraph: "And the fifth way is to be Strong, to Dominate and to Lead." This makes little sense, as a topic sentence for a concluding paragraph, because the sentences before them merely enumerated the other ways of "Getting Respect." No, if I were to merely glance at this essay, I would conclude that the conclusion is either very abrupt, well hidden, very long or very short, or some combination of these. On the possibility of the conclusion being long, I search and find that the paragraph before begins with "Then also if you are in any doubt as to what they want of you, you can always change the scene." But this seems to me like more of the same—another of what my college writing instructors would have called "body paragraphs."

The question of how it leaves me feeling is important, I think, perhaps the most important question I can ask about a conclusion. Because if it's the job of the introduction to take me from the Title to the Body of an essay, then it is the function of conclusions to remove me from the body of the essay, back into the world, with some new sense, feeling, or thought. But it's not just anywhere in the world. I should be delivered, as it were, to a particular place, or at least unleashed in a particular direction.

So let's look at the conclusion for Belloc's essay one more time, and consider this: where does he want me to go, what does he want me to do? If my answers to these questions turn up nothing, then I should ask myself, what does he want me to think, or to believe—what, finally, does he want me to feel:

> And the fifth way is to be Strong, to Dominate and to Lead. To be one of the Makers of this world, one of the Builders. To have the more Powerful Will. To arouse in all around you by mere Force of Personality a feeling that they must Obey. But I do not know how this is done.

The tone of this final enumerating paragraph turns suddenly dark and serious, in a way. Or satirical, or perhaps revelatory, when he writes about having the "more Powerful Will," culminating in the notion of obedience. I am left with a sense here, that this essay was not entirely about what it was about. That it has become something else entirely; and that this essay is a kind of commentary on something universal to the experience of getting respect. It leaves me thinking. I find that with a little reflection, the conclusion was here all along—but it was hidden! But the essayist has left me chewing on it; he hasn't spelled it out directly, spoon feeding me like one would a child, but it has become clear enough.

I would say that, in response to my original question, that the conclusion and the body of this essay are seamless. That they are so wholly integrated that it seems almost, to one who is not quite paying attention, that there is no conclusion at all. But upon taking a closer look...

Goldfish

A. A. Milne

Let us talk about—well, anything you will. Goldfish, for instance.

Goldfish are a symbol of old-world tranquility or mid-Victorian futility according to their position in the home. Outside the home, in that wild state from which civilization has dragged them, they may have stood for dare-devil courage or constancy or devotion; I cannot tell. I may only speak of them now as I find them, which is in the garden or in the drawing-room. In their lily-leaved pool, sunk deep in the old flagged terrace, upon whose borders the blackbird whistles his early-morning song, they remind me of sundials and lavender and old delightful things. But in their cheap glass bowl upon the three-legged table, above which the cloth-covered canary maintains a stolid silence, they remind me of antimacassars and horsehair sofas and all that is depressing. It is hard that the goldfish himself should have so little choice in the matter. Goldfish look pretty in the terrace pond, yet I doubt if it was the need for prettiness which brought them there. Rather the need for some thing to throw things to. No one of the initiate can sit in front of Nature's most wonderful effect, the sea, without wishing to throw stones into it, the physical pleasure of the effort and the aesthetic pleasure of the splash combining to produce perfect contentment. So by the margin of the pool the same desires stir within one, and because ants' eggs do not splash, and look untidy on the surface of the water, there must be a gleam of gold and silver to put the crown upon one's pleasure.

Perhaps when you have been feeding the goldfish you have not thought of it like that. But at least you must have wondered why, of all diets, they should prefer ants' eggs. Ants' eggs are, I should say, the very last thing which one would take to without argument. It must be an acquired taste, and, this being so, one naturally asks oneself how goldfish came to acquire it.

I suppose (but I am lamentably ignorant on these as on all other matters) that there was a time when goldfish lived a wild free life of their own. They roamed the sea or the river, or whatever it was, fighting for existence, and Nature showed them, as she always does, the food which suited them. Now I have often come across ants' nests in my travels, but never when swimming. In seas and rivers, pools and lakes, I have wandered, but Nature has never put ants' eggs in my way. No doubt—it would be only right—the goldfish has a keener eye than I have for these things, but if they had been there, should I have missed them so completely? I think not, for if they had been there, they must have been there in great quantities. I can imagine a goldfish slowly acquiring the taste for them through the centuries, but only if other food were denied to him, only if, wherever he went, ants' eggs, ants' eggs, ants' eggs drifted down the stream to him.

Yet, since it would seem that he has acquired the taste, it can only be that the taste has come to him with captivity—has been forced upon him, I should have said. The old wild goldfish (this is my theory) was a more terrible beast than we think. Given his proper diet, he could not have been kept within the limits of the terrace pool. He would have been unsuited to domestic life; he would have dragged in the shrieking child as she leaned to feed him. As the result of many experiments ants' eggs were given him to keep him thin (you can see for yourself what a bloodless diet it is), ants' eggs were given him to quell his spirit; and just as a man, if he has sufficient colds, can get up a passion even for ammoniated quinine, so the goldfish has grown in captivity to welcome the once-hated omelet.

Let us consider now the case of the goldfish in the house. His diet is the same, but how different his surroundings! If his bowl is placed on a table in the middle of the floor, he has but to flash his tail once and he has been all round the drawing-room. The drawing-room may not seem much to you, but to him this impressionist picture through the curved glass must be amazing. Let not the outdoor goldfish boast of his freedom. What does he, in his little world of water-lily roots, know of the vista upon vista which opens to his more happy brother as he passes jauntily from china dog to ottoman and from ottoman to Henry's father? Ah, here is life! It may be that in the course of years he will get used to it, even bored by it; indeed, for that reason I always advocate giving him a glance at the dining-room or the bedrooms on Wednesdays and Saturdays; but his first day in the bowl must be the opening of an undreamed-of heaven to him.

Again, what an adventurous life is his. At any moment a cat may climb up and fetch him out, a child may upset him, grown-ups may neglect to feed him or to change his water. The temptation to take him up and massage him must be irresistible to outsiders. All these dangers the goldfish in the pond avoids; he lives a sheltered and unexciting life, and when he wants to die he dies unnoticed, unregretted, but for his brother the tears and the solemn funeral.

Yes; now that I have thought it out, I can see that I was wrong in calling the indoor goldfish a symbol of mid-Victorian futility. An article of this sort is no good if it does not teach the writer something as well as his readers. I recognize him now as the symbol of enterprise and endurance, of restlessness and Post-Impressionism. He is not mid-Victorian, he is Fifth Georgian.

Which is all I want to say about goldfish.

Assertion and Support

John Pfannkuchen

I often find myself in the company of people who just say things, and am left with the distinct impression that the others standing in the same room might just take the things being said at face value. There seems to be a reticence toward the idea of challenge, or question-asking in these circumstances, or perhaps it's merely the motive of self preservation on the part of the listener, not wanting to put their foot into something they might not well get out of. I can sympathize. But with the person doing the speaking, making bold assertions, like, "The economy is doing great," and any statements with "Western Culture" as the subject, or that begin with "Throughout time," or "I read a study," and the like. Hopelessly vague, unattributed, and unaccountable are the impressions left on me. Now—I know what you're thinking—I'm a terrible conversationalist. And that's probably true, and anyways, what does it matter where I got the thing I'm saying to you now? So long as one of us is convinced of its veracity.

Well dear reader—I will tell you—sometimes people say ridiculous things for affect, and other times people say ridiculous things dressed up as reasonable; I believe that the ability to just say a thing without reason or evidence has all but ruined regular conversation. People will just say anything nowadays, including perfectly contradictory things in the same breath, and it's fine because no one is listening anyway. That's the real casualty of meaningless talk—the loss of interest—no one wants to listen to anyone anymore because as I previous stated, people "just talk", making sounds with their mouths, more or less without intention or purpose.

In writing it is the same as in speaking. In writing we call it a thesis—and in speaking a proposition. I believe that one should think before they speak, so it follows that one should think before they write. Which means that if one is to form a thesis in writing, it should be formed after the bulk of the essay has already been written, so that the writing itself will buy the essayist time to make up their mind.

By the way, even in writing I prefer the word proposition to thesis, since both words mean the same thing, but while proposition is clear English, the other is pompous and technical sounding, and tends to send one into fits.

A proposition differs from an assertion in that it is felt less strongly than an assertion, that is, the author admits that it is a merely a proposition, and not a fact. However, in the offering of a proposition, the essayist will have the opportunity to make certain assertions of fact, opinion, or observation, in support of their proposition. The way I remember it is this: propositions are supported by assertions, assertions are supported by facts, and facts are supported by observation.

So, let's say I read something. And I see or experienced something. And the thing I read, or the memory I have, gives me an idea. Well, I need a way of telling the reader about the connection between my experience and my idea, don't I?

So I assert an idea. This is where I get into trouble. I have said something bold, that the reader may find surprising or silly. Can't I just leave it at that, and expect you, my dear reader, to trust in my words? I don't even feel the need to show you how I came upon this idea, but instead I offer to spend a few hundred words repeating in various ways that I am definitely right, trustworthy, and anyone who dare doubt me is a nincompoop or a Communist.

But I don't think my tactics will hold water for long. I've learned to assume that even quiet and agreeable people, when reading or listening, will wonder quietly, "Is that true? How do you know?" So I've gotten into the habit of explaining myself, so as not to leave the reader with the impression that I should always be believed at face value (I am often wrong).

So I've gotten into the habit of sharing how I had came up with the proposition in the first place, starting from the original observation that was made, and then moving through the assertions, and finally to my proposition, showing the entire chain of logic and deduction to the reader. I try to lay this all out quite methodically. The support can come in any form, really. It can be reasoning, a reference to something we read or saw or a historical fact. It can be anything. But I have to support my assertions somehow.

It may be enough for some to just assault the poor reader with assertion after assertion, until the reader waves a white flag of surrender; and although I believe many great writers may wear the reader down, convince the reader to accept any proposition made with little to no convincing other than sheer force of personality, it hasn't worked for me yet.

The Stolen White Elephant

Mark Twain

1

The following curious history was related to me by a chance railway acquaintance. He was a gentleman more than seventy years of age, and his thoroughly good and gentle face and earnest and sincere manner imprinted the unmistakable stamp of truth upon every statement which fell from his lips. He said:

You know in what reverence the royal white elephant of Siam is held by the people of that country. You know it is sacred to kings, only kings may possess it, and that it is, indeed, in a measure even superior to kings, since it receives not merely honor but worship. Very well; five years ago, when the troubles concerning the frontier line arose between Great Britain and Siam, it was presently manifest that Siam had been in the wrong. Therefore every reparation was quickly made, and the British representative stated that he was satisfied and the past should be forgotten. This greatly relieved the King of Siam, and partly as a token of gratitude, but partly also, perhaps, to wipe out any little remaining vestige of unpleasantness which England might feel toward him, he wished to send the Queen a present—the sole sure way of propitiating an enemy, according to Oriental ideas. This present ought not only to be a royal one, but transcendently royal. Wherefore, what offering could be so meet as that of a white elephant? My position in the Indian civil service was such that I was deemed peculiarly worthy of the honor of conveying the present to her Majesty. A ship was fitted out for me and my servants and the officers and attendants of the elephant, and in due time I arrived in New York harbor and placed my royal charge in admirable quarters in Jersey City. It was necessary to remain awhile in order to recruit the animal's health before resuming the voyage.

All went well during a fortnight—then my calamities began. The white elephant was stolen! I was called up at dead of night and informed of this fearful misfortune. For some moments I was beside myself with terror and anxiety; I was helpless. Then I grew calmer and collected my faculties. I soon saw my course—for, indeed, there was but the one course for an intelligent man to pursue. Late as it was, I flew to New York and got a policeman to conduct me to the headquarters of the detective force. Fortunately I arrived in time, though the chief of the force, the celebrated Inspector Blunt was just on the point of leaving for his home. He was a man of middle size and compact frame, and when he was thinking deeply he had a way of knitting his brows and tapping his forehead reflectively with his finger, which impressed you at once with the conviction that you stood in the presence of a person of no common order. The very sight of him gave me confidence and made me hopeful. I stated my errand. It did not flurry him in the least; it had no more visible effect upon his iron self-possession than if I had told him somebody had stolen my dog. He motioned me to a seat, and said, calmly:

"Allow me to think a moment, please."

So saying, he sat down at his office table and leaned his head upon his hand. Several clerks were at work at the other end of the room; the scratching of their pens was all the sound I heard during the next six or seven minutes. Meantime the inspector sat there, buried in thought. Finally he raised his head, and there was that in the firm lines of his face which showed me that his brain had done its work and his plan was made. Said he—and his voice was low and impressive:

"This is no ordinary case. Every step must be warily taken; each step must be made sure before the next is ventured. And secrecy must be observed—secrecy profound and absolute. Speak to no one about the matter, not even the reporters. I will take care of them; I will see that they get only what it may suit my ends to let them know." He touched a bell; a youth appeared. "Alaric, tell the reporters to remain for the present." The boy retired. "Now let us proceed to business—

and systematically. Nothing can be accomplished in this trade of mine without strict and minute method."

He took a pen and some paper. "Now—name of the elephant?"

"Hassan Ben Ali Ben Selim Abdallah Mohammed Moisé Alhammal Jamsetjejeebhoy Dhuleep Sultan Ebu Bhudpoor."

"Very well. Given name?"

"Jumbo."

"Very well. Place of birth?"

"The capital city of Siam."

"Parents living?"

"No—dead."

"Had they any other issue besides this one?"

"None. He was an only child."

"Very well. These matters are sufficient under that head. Now please describe the elephant, and leave out no particular, however insignificant—that is, insignificant from your point of view. To men in my profession there are no insignificant particulars; they do not exist."

I described, he wrote. When I was done, he said:

"Now listen. If I have made any mistakes, correct me."

He read as follows:

"Height, 19 feet; length from apex of forehead to insertion of tail, 26 feet; length of trunk, 16 feet; length of tail, 6 feet; total length, including trunk, and tail, 48 feet; length of tusks, 9 1/2 feet; ears keeping with these dimensions; footprint resembles the mark left when one up-ends a barrel in the snow; color of the elephant, a dull white; has a hole the size of a plate in each ear for the insertion of jewelry and possesses the habit in a remarkable degree of squirting water upon spectators and of maltreating with his trunk not only such persons as he is acquainted with, but even entire strangers; limps slightly with his right hind leg, and has a small scar in his left armpit caused by a former boil; had on, when stolen, a castle containing seats for fifteen persons, and a gold-cloth saddle-blanket the size of an ordinary carpet."

There were no mistakes. The inspector touched the bell, handed the description to Alaric, and said:

"Have fifty thousand copies of this printed at once and mailed to every detective office and pawnbroker's shop on the continent." Alaric retired. "There—so far, so good. Next, I must have a photograph of the property."

I gave him one. He examined it critically, and said:

"It must do, since we can do no better; but he has his trunk curled up and tucked into his mouth. That is unfortunate, and is calculated to mislead, for of course he does not usually have it in that position." He touched his bell.

"Alaric, have fifty thousand copies of this photograph made the first thing in the morning, and mail them with the descriptive circulars."

Alaric retired to execute his orders. The inspector said:

"It will be necessary to offer a reward, of course. Now as to the amount?"

"What sum would you suggest?"

"To begin with, I should say—well, twenty-five thousand dollars. It is an intricate and difficult business; there are a thousand avenues of escape and opportunities of concealment. These thieves have friends and pals everywhere—"

"Bless me, do you know who they are?"

The wary face, practiced in concealing the thoughts and feelings within, gave me no token, nor yet the replying words, so quietly uttered:

"Never mind about that. I may, and I may not. We generally gather a pretty shrewd inkling of who our man is by the manner of his work and the size of the game he goes after. We are not dealing with a pickpocket or a hall thief now, make up your mind to that. This property was not 'lifted' by a novice. But, as I was saying, considering the amount of travel which will have to be done, and the diligence with which the thieves will cover up their traces as they move along, twenty-five thousand may be too small a sum to offer, yet I think it worth while to start with that."

So we determined upon that figure as a beginning. Then this man, whom nothing escaped which could by any possibility be made to serve as a clue, said:

"There are cases in detective history to show that criminals have been detected through peculiarities, in their appetites. Now, what does this elephant eat, and how much?"

"Well, as to what he eats—he will eat anything. He will eat a man, he will eat a Bible—he will eat anything between a man and a Bible."

"Good very good, indeed, but too general. Details are necessary—details are the only valuable things in our trade. Very well—as to men. At one meal—or, if you prefer, during one day—how many men will he eat, if fresh?"

"He would not care whether they were fresh or not; at a single meal he would eat five ordinary men."

"Very good; five men; we will put that down. What nationalities would he prefer?"

"He is indifferent about nationalities. He prefers acquaintances, but is not prejudiced against strangers."

"Very good. Now, as to Bibles. How many Bibles would he eat at a meal?"

"He would eat an entire edition."

"It is hardly succinct enough. Do you mean the ordinary octavo, or the family illustrated?"

"I think he would be indifferent to illustrations that is, I think he would not value illustrations above simple letterpress."

"No, you do not get my idea. I refer to bulk. The ordinary octavo Bible weighs about two pounds and a half, while the great quarto with the illustrations weighs ten or twelve. How many Dore Bibles would he eat at a meal?"

"If you knew this elephant, you could not ask. He would take what they had."

"Well, put it in dollars and cents, then. We must get at it somehow. The Dore costs a hundred dollars a copy, Russia leather, beveled."

"He would require about fifty thousand dollars worth—say an edition of five hundred copies."

"Now that is more exact. I will put that down. Very well; he likes men and Bibles; so far, so good. What else will he eat? I want particulars."

"He will leave Bibles to eat bricks, he will leave bricks to eat bottles, he will leave bottles to eat clothing, he will leave clothing to eat cats, he will leave cats to eat oysters, he will leave oysters to eat ham, he will leave ham to eat sugar, he will leave sugar to eat pie, he will leave pie to eat potatoes, he will leave potatoes to eat bran; he will leave bran to eat hay, he will leave hay to eat oats, he will leave oats to eat rice, for he was mainly raised on it. There is nothing whatever that he will not eat but European butter, and he would eat that if he could taste it."

"Very good. General quantity at a meal—say about—"

"Well, anywhere from a quarter to half a ton."

"And he drinks—"

"Everything that is fluid. Milk, water, whiskey, molasses, castor oil, camphene, carbolic acid—it is no use to go into particulars; whatever fluid occurs to you set it down. He will drink anything that is fluid, except European coffee."

"Very good. As to quantity?"

"Put it down five to fifteen barrels—his thirst varies; his other appetites do not."

"These things are unusual. They ought to furnish quite good clues toward tracing him."

He touched the bell.

"Alaric; summon Captain Burns."

Burns appeared. Inspector Blunt unfolded the whole matter to him, detail by detail. Then he said in the clear, decisive tones of a man whose plans are clearly defined in his head and who is accustomed to command:

"Captain Burns, detail Detectives Jones, Davis, Halsey, Bates, and Hackett to shadow the elephant."

"Yes, sir."

"Detail Detectives Moses, Dakin, Murphy, Rogers, Tupper, Higgins, and Bartholomew to shadow the thieves."

"Yes, sir."

"Place a strong guard—A guard of thirty picked men, with a relief of thirty—over the place from whence the elephant was stolen, to keep strict watch there night and day, and allow none to approach—except reporters—without written authority from me."

"Yes, sir."

"Place detectives in plain clothes in the railway; steamship, and ferry depots, and upon all roadways leading out of Jersey City, with orders to search all suspicious persons."

"Yes, sir."

"Furnish all these men with photograph and accompanying description of the elephant, and instruct them to search all trains and outgoing ferryboats and other vessels."

"Yes, sir."

"If the elephant should be found, let him be seized, and the information forwarded to me by telegraph."

"Yes, sir."

"Let me be informed at once if any clues should be found—footprints of the animal, or anything of that kind."

"Yes, sir."

"Get an order commanding the harbor police to patrol the frontages vigilantly."

"Yes, sir."

"Dispatch detectives in plain clothes over all the railways, north as far as Canada, west as far as Ohio, south as far as Washington."

"Yes, sir."

"Place experts in all the telegraph offices to listen to all messages; and let them require that all cipher dispatches be interpreted to them."

"Yes, sir."

"Let all these things be done with the utmost's secrecy—mind, the most impenetrable secrecy."

"Yes, sir."

"Report to me promptly at the usual hour."

"Yes, Sir."

"Go!"

"Yes, sir."

He was gone.

Inspector Blunt was silent and thoughtful a moment, while the fire in his eye cooled down and faded out. Then he turned to me and said in a placid voice:

"I am not given to boasting, it is not my habit; but—we shall find the elephant."

I shook him warmly by the hand and thanked him; and I FELT my thanks, too. The more I had seen of the man the more I liked him and the more I admired him and marveled over the mysterious wonders of his profession. Then we parted for the night, and I went home with a far happier heart than I had carried with me to his office.

2

Next morning it was all in the newspapers, in the minutest detail. It even had additions—consisting of Detective This, Detective That, and Detective The Other's "Theory" as to how the robbery was done, who the robbers were, and whither they had flown with their booty. There were eleven of these theories, and they covered all the possibilities; and this single fact shows what independent thinkers detectives are. No two theories were alike, or even much resembled each other, save in one striking particular, and in that one all the other eleven theories were absolutely agreed. That was, that although the rear of my building was torn out and the only door remained locked, the elephant had not been removed through the rent, but by some other (undiscovered) outlet. All agreed that the robbers had made that rent only to mislead the detectives. That never would have occurred to me or to any other layman, perhaps, but it had not deceived the detectives for a moment. Thus, what I had supposed was the only thing that had no mystery about it was in fact the very thing I had gone furthest astray in. The eleven theories all named the supposed robbers, but no two named the same robbers; the total number of suspected persons was thirty-seven. The various newspaper accounts all closed with the most important opinion of all—that of Chief Inspector Blunt. A portion of this statement read as follows:

The chief knows who the two principals are, namely, "Brick" Duffy and "Red" McFadden. Ten days before the robbery was achieved he was already aware that it was to be attempted, and had quietly proceeded to shadow these two noted villains; but unfortunately on the night in question their track was lost, and before it could be found again the bird was flown—that is, the elephant.

Duffy and McFadden are the boldest scoundrels in the profession; the chief has reasons for believing that they are the men who stole the stove out of the detective headquarters on a bitter night last winter—in consequence of which the chief and every detective present were in the hands of the physicians before morning, some with frozen feet, others with frozen fingers, ears, and other members.

When I read the first half of that I was more astonished than ever at the wonderful sagacity of this strange man. He not only saw everything in the present with a clear eye, but even the future could not be hidden from him. I was soon at his office, and said I could not help wishing he had had those men arrested, and so prevented the trouble and loss; but his reply was simple and unanswerable:

"It is not our province to prevent crime, but to punish it. We cannot punish it until it is committed."

I remarked that the secrecy with which we had begun had been marred by the newspapers; not only all our facts but all our plans and purposes had been revealed; even all the suspected persons had been named; these would doubtless disguise themselves now, or go into hiding.

"Let them. They will find that when I am ready for them my hand will descend upon them, in their secret places, as unerringly as the hand of fate. As to the newspapers, we must keep in with them. Fame, reputation, constant public mention—these are the detective's bread and butter. He must publish his facts, else he will be supposed to have none; he must publish his theory, for nothing is so strange or striking as a detective's theory, or brings him so much wondering respect; we must publish our plans, for these the journals insist upon having, and we could not deny them without offending. We must constantly show the public what we are doing, or they will believe we are doing nothing. It is much pleasanter to have a newspaper say, 'Inspector Blunt's ingenious and extraordinary theory is as follows,' than to have it say some harsh thing, or, worse still, some sarcastic one."

"I see the force of what you say. But I noticed that in one part of your remarks in the papers this morning you refused to reveal your opinion upon a certain minor point."

"Yes, we always do that; it has a good effect. Besides, I had not formed any opinion on that point, anyway."

I deposited a considerable sum of money with the inspector, to meet current expenses, and sat down to wait for news. We were expecting the telegrams to begin to arrive at any moment now. Meantime I reread the newspapers and also our descriptive circular, and observed that our twenty-five thousand dollars reward seemed to be offered only to detectives. I said I thought it ought to be offered to anybody who would catch the elephant. The inspector said:

"It is the detectives who will find the elephant; hence the reward will go to the right place. If other people found the animal, it would only be by watching the detectives and taking advantage of clues and indications stolen from them, and that would entitle the detectives to the reward, after all. The proper office of a reward is to stimulate the men who deliver up their time and their trained sagacities to this sort of work, and not to confer benefits upon chance citizens who stumble upon a capture without having earned the benefits by their own merits and labors."

This was reasonable enough, certainly. Now the telegraphic machine in the corner began to click, and the following dispatch was the result:

FLOWER STATION, N. Y., 7.30 A.M. Have got a clue. Found a succession of deep tracks across a farm near here. Followed them two miles east without result; think elephant went west. Shall now shadow him in that direction. DARLEY, Detective.

"Darley's one of the best men on the force," said the inspector. "We shall hear from him again before long."

Telegram No. 2 came:

BARKER'S, N. J., 7.40 A.M. Just arrived. Glass factory broken open here during night, and eight hundred bottles taken. Only water in large quantity near here is five miles distant. Shall strike for there. Elephant will be thirsty. Bottles were empty. BAKER, Detective.

"That promises well, too," said the inspector.

"I told you the creature's appetites would not be bad clues."

Telegram No. 3:

TAYLORVILLE, L. I. 8.15 A.M. A haystack near here disappeared during night. Probably eaten. Have got a clue, and am off. HUBBARD, Detective.

"How he does move around!" said the inspector "I knew we had a difficult job on hand, but we shall catch him yet."

FLOWER STATION, N. Y., 9 A.M. Shadowed the tracks three miles westward. Large, deep, and ragged. Have just met a farmer who says they are not elephant-tracks. Says they are holes where he dug up saplings for shade-trees when ground was frozen last winter. Give me orders how to proceed. DARLEY, Detective.

"Aha! a confederate of the thieves! The thing, grows warm," said the inspector.

He dictated the following telegram to Darley:

Arrest the man and force him to name his pals. Continue to follow the tracks to the Pacific, if necessary. Chief BLUNT.

Next telegram:

CONEY POINT, PA., 8.45 A.M. Gas office broken open here during night and three months' unpaid gas bills taken. Have got a clue and am away. MURPHY, Detective.

"Heavens!" said the inspector; "would he eat gas bills?"

"Through ignorance—yes; but they cannot support life. At least, unassisted."

Now came this exciting telegram:

IRONVILLE, N. Y., 9.30 A.M. Just arrived. This village in consternation. Elephant passed through here at five this morning. Some say he went east some say west, some north, some south—but all say they did not wait to notice, particularly. He killed a horse; have secured a piece of it for a clue. Killed it with his trunk; from style of blow, think he struck it left-handed. From position in which horse lies, think elephant traveled northward along line of Berkley Railway. Has four and a half hours' start, but I move on his track at once. HAWES, Detective

I uttered exclamations of joy. The inspector was as self-contained as a graven image. He calmly touched his bell.

"Alaric, send Captain Burns here."

Burns appeared.

"How many men are ready for instant orders?"

"Ninety-six, sir."

"Send them north at once. Let them concentrate along the line of the Berkley road north of Ironville."

"Yes, sir."

"Let them conduct their movements with the utmost secrecy. As fast as others are at liberty, hold them for orders."

"Yes, sir."

"Go!"

"Yes, sir."

Presently came another telegram:

SAGE CORNERS, N. Y., 10.30. Just arrived. Elephant passed through here at 8.15. All escaped from the town but a policeman. Apparently elephant did not strike at policeman, but at the lamp-post. Got both. I have secured a portion of the policeman as clue. STUMM, Detective.

"So the elephant has turned westward," said the inspector. "However, he will not escape, for my men are scattered all over that region."

The next telegram said:

GLOVER'S, 11.15 Just arrived. Village deserted, except sick and aged. Elephant passed through three-quarters of an hour ago. The anti-temperance mass-meeting was in session; he put his trunk in at a window and washed it out with water from cistern. Some swallowed it—since dead; several drowned. Detectives Cross and O'Shaughnessy were passing through town, but going south—so missed elephant. Whole region for many miles around in terror—people flying from their homes. Wherever they turn they meet elephant, and many are killed. BRANT, Detective.

I could have shed tears, this havoc so distressed me. But the inspector only said:

"You see—we are closing in on him. He feels our presence; he has turned eastward again."

Yet further troublous news was in store for us. The telegraph brought this:

HOGANSPORT, 12.19. Just arrived. Elephant passed through half an hour ago, creating wildest fright and excitement. Elephant raged around streets; two plumbers going by, killed one—other escaped. Regret general. O'FLAHERTY, Detective.

"Now he is right in the midst of my men," said the inspector. "Nothing can save him."

A succession of telegrams came from detectives who were scattered through New Jersey and Pennsylvania, and who were following clues consisting of ravaged barns, factories, and Sunday-school libraries, with high hopes-hopes amounting to certainties, indeed. The inspector said:

"I wish I could communicate with them and order them north, but that is impossible. A detective only visits a telegraph office to send his report; then he is off again, and you don't know where to put your hand on him."

Now came this dispatch:

BRIDGEPORT, CT., 12.15. Barnum offers rate of $4,000 a year for exclusive privilege of using elephant as traveling advertising medium from now till detectives find him. Wants to paste circus-posters on him. Desires immediate answer. BOGGS, Detective.

"That is perfectly absurd!" I exclaimed.

"Of course it is," said the inspector. "Evidently Mr. Barnum, who thinks he is so sharp, does not know me—but I know him."

Then he dictated this answer to the dispatch:

Mr. Barnum's offer declined. Make it $7,000 or nothing. Chief BLUNT.

"There. We shall not have to wait long for an answer. Mr. Barnum is not at home; he is in the telegraph office—it is his way when he has business on hand. Inside of three—"

Done.—P. T. BARNUM.

So interrupted the clicking telegraphic instrument. Before I could make a comment upon this extraordinary episode, the following dispatch carried my thoughts into another and very distressing channel:

BOLIVIA, N. Y., 12.50. Elephant arrived here from the south and passed through toward the forest at 11.50, dispersing a funeral on the way, and diminishing the mourners by two. Citizens fired some small cannon-balls into him, and then fled. Detective Burke and I arrived ten minutes later, from the north, but mistook some excavations for footprints, and so lost a good deal of time; but at last we struck the right trail and followed it to the woods. We then got down on our hands and knees and continued to keep a sharp eye on the track, and so shadowed it into the brush. Burke was in advance. Unfortunately the animal had stopped to rest; therefore, Burke having his head down, intent upon the track, butted up against the elephant's hind legs before he was aware of his vicinity. Burke instantly arose to his feet, seized the tail, and exclaimed joyfully, "I claim the re—" but got no further, for a single blow of the huge trunk laid the brave fellow's fragments low in death. I fled rearward, and the elephant turned and shadowed me to the edge of the wood, making tremendous speed, and I should inevitably have been lost, but that the remains of the funeral providentially intervened again and diverted his attention. I have just learned that nothing of that funeral is now left; but this is no loss, for there is abundance of material for another. Meantime, the elephant has disappeared again. MULROONEY, Detective.

We heard no news except from the diligent and confident detectives scattered about New Jersey, Pennsylvania, Delaware, and Virginia—who were all following fresh and encouraging clues—until shortly after 2 P.M., when this telegram came:

BAXTER CENTER, 2.15. Elephant been here, plastered over with circus-bills, and he broke up a revival, striking down and damaging many who were on the point of entering upon a better life. Citizens penned him up and established a guard. When Detective Brown and I arrived, some time after, we entered enclosure and proceeded to identify elephant by photograph and description. All marks tallied exactly except one, which we could not see—the boil-scar under armpit. To make sure, Brown crept under to look, and was immediately brained—that is, head crushed and destroyed, though nothing issued from debris. All fled so did elephant, striking right and left with much effect. Has escaped, but left bold blood-track from cannon-wounds. Rediscovery certain. He broke southward, through a dense forest. BRENT, Detective.

That was the last telegram. At nightfall a fog shut down which was so dense that objects but three feet away could not be discerned. This lasted all night. The ferry-boats and even the omnibuses had to stop running.

3

Next morning the papers were as full of detective theories as before; they had all our tragic facts in detail also, and a great many more which they had received from their telegraphic correspondents. Column after column was occupied, a third of its way down, with glaring head-lines, which it made my heart sick to read. Their general tone was like this:

THE WHITE ELEPHANT AT LARGE! HE MOVES UPON HIS FATAL MARCH! WHOLE VILLAGES DESERTED BY THEIR FRIGHT-STRICKEN OCCUPANTS! PALE TERROR GOES BEFORE HIM, DEATH AND DEVASTATION FOLLOW AFTER! AFTER THESE, THE DETECTIVES! BARNS DESTROYED, FACTORIES GUTTED, HARVESTS DEVOURED, PUBLIC ASSEMBLAGES DISPERSED, ACCOMPANIED BY SCENES OF CARNAGE IMPOSSIBLE TO DESCRIBE! THEORIES OF THIRTY-FOUR OF THE MOST DISTINGUISHED DETECTIVES ON THE FORCE! THEORY OF CHIEF BLUNT!

"There!" said Inspector Blunt, almost betrayed into excitement, "this is magnificent! This is the greatest windfall that any detective organization ever had. The fame of it will travel to the ends of the earth, and endure to the end of time, and my name with it."

But there was no joy for me. I felt as if I had committed all those red crimes, and that the elephant was only my irresponsible agent. And how the list had grown! In one place he had "interfered with an election and killed five repeaters." He had followed this act with the destruction of two pool fellows, named O'Donohue and McFlannigan, who had "found a refuge in the home of the oppressed of all lands only the day before, and were in the act of exercising for the first time the noble right of American citizens at the polls, when stricken down by the relentless hand of the Scourge of Siam." In another, he had "found a crazy sensation-preacher preparing his next season's heroic attacks on the dance, the theater, and other things which can't strike back, and had stepped on him." And in still another place he had "killed a lightning-rod agent." And so the list went on, growing redder and redder, and more and more heartbreaking. Sixty persons had been killed, and two hundred and forty wounded. All the accounts bore just testimony to the activity and devotion of the detectives, and all closed with the remark that "three hundred thousand citizens and four detectives saw the dread creature, and two of the latter he destroyed."

I dreaded to hear the telegraphic instrument begin to click again. By and by the messages began to pour in, but I was happily disappointed in their nature. It was soon apparent that all trace of the elephant was lost. The fog had enabled him to search out a good hiding-place unobserved. Telegrams from the most absurdly distant points reported that a dim vast mass had been glimpsed there through the fog at such and such an hour, and was "undoubtedly the elephant." This dim vast mass had been glimpsed in New Haven, in New Jersey, in Pennsylvania, in interior New York, in Brooklyn, and even in the city of New York itself! But in all cases the dim vast mass had vanished quickly and left no trace. Every detective of the large force scattered over this huge extent of country sent his hourly report, and each and every one of them had a clue, and was shadowing something, and was hot upon the heels of it.

But the day passed without other result.

The next day the same.

The next just the same.

The newspaper reports began to grow monotonous with facts that amounted to nothing, clues which led to nothing, and theories which had nearly exhausted the elements which surprise and delight and dazzle.

By advice of the inspector I doubled the reward.

Four more dull days followed. Then came a bitter blow to the poor, hard-working detectives—the journalists declined to print their theories, and coldly said, "Give us a rest."

Two weeks after the elephant's disappearance I raised the reward to seventy-five thousand dollars by the inspector's advice. It was a great sum, but I felt that I would rather sacrifice my whole private fortune than lose my credit with my government. Now that the detectives were in adversity, the newspapers turned upon them, and began to fling the most stinging sarcasms at them. This gave the minstrels an idea, and they dressed themselves as detectives and hunted the elephant on the stage in the most extravagant way. The caricaturists made pictures of detectives scanning the country with spy-glasses, while the elephant, at their backs, stole apples out of their pockets. And they made all sorts of ridiculous pictures of the detective badge—you have seen that badge printed in gold on the back of detective novels no doubt, it is a wide-staring eye, with the legend, "WE NEVER SLEEP." When detectives called for a drink, the would-be facetious barkeeper resurrected an obsolete form of expression and said, "Will you have an eye-opener?" All the air was thick with sarcasms.

But there was one man who moved calm, untouched, unaffected, through it all. It was that heart of oak, the chief inspector. His brave eye never drooped, his serene confidence never wavered. He always said:

"Let them rail on; he laughs best who laughs last."

My admiration for the man grew into a species of worship. I was at his side always. His office had become an unpleasant place to me, and now became daily more and more so. Yet if he could endure it I meant to do so also—at least, as long as I could. So I came regularly, and stayed—the only outsider who seemed to be capable of it. Everybody wondered how I could; and often it seemed to me that I must desert, but at such times I looked into that calm and apparently unconscious face, and held my ground.

About three weeks after the elephant's disappearance I was about to say, one morning, that I should have to strike my colors and retire, when the great detective arrested the thought by proposing one more superb and masterly move.

This was to compromise with the robbers. The fertility of this man's invention exceeded anything I have ever seen, and I have had a wide intercourse with the world's finest minds. He said he was confident he could compromise for one hundred thousand dollars and recover the elephant. I said I believed I could scrape the amount together, but what would become of the poor detectives who had worked so faithfully? He said:

"In compromises they always get half."

This removed my only objection. So the inspector wrote two notes, in this form:

DEAR MADAM,—Your husband can make a large sum of money (and be entirely protected from the law) by making an immediate, appointment with me. Chief BLUNT.

He sent one of these by his confidential messenger to the "reputed wife" of Brick Duffy, and the other to the reputed wife of Red McFadden.

Within the hour these offensive answers came:

YE OWLD FOOL: brick McDuffys bin ded 2 yere. BRIDGET MAHONEY.

CHIEF BAT,—Red McFadden is hung and in heving 18 month. Any Ass but a detective know that. MARY O'HOOLIGAN.

"I had long suspected these facts," said the inspector; "this testimony proves the unerring accuracy of my instinct."

The moment one resource failed him he was ready with another. He immediately wrote an advertisement for the morning papers, and I kept a copy of it:

A.—xwblv.242 N. Tjnd—fz328wmlg. Ozpo,—; 2m! ogw. Mum

He said that if the thief was alive this would bring him to the usual rendezvous. He further explained that the usual rendezvous was a place where all business affairs between detectives and criminals were conducted. This meeting would take place at twelve the next night.

We could do nothing till then, and I lost no time in getting out of the office, and was grateful indeed for the privilege.

At eleven the next night I brought one hundred thousand dollars in bank-notes and put them into the chief's hands, and shortly afterward he took his leave, with the brave old undimmed confidence in his eye. An almost intolerable hour dragged to a close; then I heard his welcome tread, and rose gasping and tottered to meet him. How his fine eyes flamed with triumph! He said:

"We've compromised! The jokers will sing a different tune to-morrow! Follow me!"

He took a lighted candle and strode down into the vast vaulted basement where sixty detectives always slept, and where a score were now playing cards to while the time. I followed close after him. He walked swiftly down to the dim remote end of the place, and just as I succumbed to the pangs of suffocation and was swooning away he stumbled and fell over the outlying members of a mighty object, and I heard him exclaim as he went down:

"Our noble profession is vindicated. Here is your elephant!"

I was carried to the office above and restored with carbolic acid. The whole detective force swarmed in, and such another season of triumphant rejoicing ensued as I had never witnessed before. The reporters were called, baskets of champagne were opened, toasts were drunk, the handshakings and congratulations were continuous and enthusiastic. Naturally the chief was the hero of the hour, and his happiness was so complete and had been so patiently and worthily and bravely won that it made me happy to see it, though I stood there a homeless beggar, my priceless charge dead, and my position in my country's service lost to me through what would always seem my fatally careless execution of a great trust. Many an eloquent eye testified its deep admiration for the chief, and many a detective's voice murmured, "Look at him—just the king of the profession; only give him a clue, it's all he wants, and there ain't anything hid that he can't find." The dividing of the fifty thousand dollars made great pleasure; when it was finished the chief made a little speech while he put his share in his pocket, in which he said, "Enjoy it, boys, for you've earned it; and, more than that, you've earned for the detective profession undying fame."

A telegram arrived, which read:

MONROE, MICH., 10 P.M. First time I've struck a telegraph office in over three weeks. Have followed those footprints, horseback, through the woods, a thousand miles to here, and they get stronger and bigger and fresher every day. Don't worry-inside of another week I'll have the elephant. This is dead sure. DARLEY, Detective.

The chief ordered three cheers for "Darley, one of the finest minds on the force," and then commanded that he be telegraphed to come home and receive his share of the reward.

So ended that marvelous episode of the stolen elephant. The newspapers were pleasant with praises once more, the next day, with one contemptible exception. This sheet said, "Great is the detective! He may be a little slow in finding a little thing like a mislaid elephant he may hunt him all day and sleep with his rotting carcass all night for three weeks, but he will find him at last if he can get the man who mislaid him to show him the place!"

Poor Hassan was lost to me forever. The cannon shots had wounded him fatally, he had crept to that unfriendly place in the fog, and there, surrounded by his enemies and in constant danger of detection, he had wasted away with hunger and suffering till death gave him peace.

The compromise cost me one hundred thousand dollars; my detective expenses were forty-two thousand dollars more; I never applied for a place again under my government; I am a ruined man and a wanderer in the earth, but my admiration for that man, whom I believe to be the greatest detective the world has ever produced, remains undimmed to this day, and will so remain unto the end.

The Library

John Pfannkuchen

After spending the better part of my life deriding and mourning those who cannot quite seem to keep up with the times, I have found myself backpedaling into the past; I used to preach the gospel of convenience through technology, through cloud computing and the Internet of things; databases and search algorithms.

No longer, however. I've since discovered, or rediscovered, the sheer speed and efficiency of strolling into a library and finding five or six books on any subject I'm curious about, and on top of finding the answer I was seeking, learning a host of other things about the matter in the offing.

This lesson was taught to me one day when I was having quite the trouble researching an essay with published articles in a scholarly database, since all the relevant articles were behind a pay wall, and everything else was too specific and therefor entirely off topic. I found the sources were nearly useless to answer the questions I had posed to them, except possible by implication—but it would have taken an expert in the subject matter to suss this out.

I would spend hours conjuring the best search terminology (which required a specialized knowledge I did not have), combing through search results, trying to determine what was relevant in each twenty page tomb and which wasn't. I'd strain my eyes at the glowing window of a laptop screen or worse yet a smart phone. I figured how convenient! I won't have to leave the comfort of my apartment, or even stand up, to copy and paste my quotations from this or that source! I'll have this essay done in no time.

But the first time I walked into a public library it was a revelation. Consider the structure of a book. It begins with a cover, and depicted on this cover is some sort of image, which allows the average person a quick understanding of what the book is about. This is ingenious! Following this is a title—a good title can convey the heart of a subject; knowing this I can peruse covers quickly—but should I find one that strikes my fancy, just inside the cover is another miracle which one cannot get on the Internet: an index, a directory of chapters, listing major topics, within the book! Running my eyes across this directory tells me whether or not the book is right for my project; no more time wasted scanning dense paragraphs on a screen! Then if I see a particularly relevant chapter, I can just turn to that page and begin reading. If the chapter is not immediately compelling, that's the test of whether or not to take the book.

But here's another feature of books—they are portable, and comprehensive, and usually they are both general and specific! One chapter will give a researcher the context they could not glean from hours of essay perusing on a scholarly database.

Here's another thing: drive, take the bus, or walk—once there the library is free. I find some librarians to be intimately familiar with the libraries, though your mileage may vary. At my local library the librarian in the reference section has an advanced degree in medieval French history, and knows all the best authors to read. A quick trip to the library and a chat with him had me set up for days of reading and learning in under an hour.

So as you can see nowadays I avoid the Internet for formal research. There are several reasons for this. First off, it seems that everyone else is using the Internet, and because of this I fear my work may not stand out among my peers. Another thing is that I find most Internet content incomplete, biased or outdated, plus the amount of scholarly, professional work is limited or very expensive. Additionally, for me at least, using the Internet encourages poor note taking practices. How often do I have to retype, or physically write down, what I find on the Internet? Seldom to never, because I can just copy and paste. I don't even read the whole article, much less read it carefully. Because of all these reasons I find that writing based on Internet research is difficult and ultimately of an inferior quality. So nowadays I take the easy way out.

I tend to read physical books first, and journals articles second. Library journal databases contain mostly academic journal articles. These are published by research universities and independent researchers. Academic journals are important for modern academics, and using them first may seem appealing. But writing may suffer from relying too early on journal articles. Using scholarly journal articles first may force a writer to combine unrelated topics.

It's better to begin with a few books. In most nonfiction books there are references to scholarly articles in the back of the book. I would scan the book to get a broad overview of the subject. Then use the references in the back of the book to understand the book better. Then I can search for the articles by author name on an online research database.

Below I have written a short guide for the would be library researcher. If you are interesting in backpedaling into the past with me, continue reading.

The first thing to do is to come prepared with your citation page perhaps in a notebook, and a bag to carry your sources (books). Bring some cash or a credit card for the photocopier.

Search the (Library) stacks with the Dewey Decimal System. With this handy system you can browse to your heart's content! There's an even more detailed version of the system in an appendix at the back of this book.

000 – Computer science, information & general works

100 – Philosophy & psychology

200 – Religion

300 – Social sciences

400 – Language

500 – Science

600 – Technology

700 – Arts & recreation

800 – Literature

900 – History & geography

Scan each book for relevance first, before checking it out. When you pull each book off the shelf begin with the cover and back. Does it seem relevant to your topic? Now look at the table of contents—that part in the front of the book that tells you all chapters and their page numbers. Look at the Part, Book, Section and Chapter headings. Do any of them jump out to you as especially interesting or relevant to your topic? If so, turn to that place and scan the first page. If it looks useful, take that book. If a book does not seem like it will be useful to you, put it back on the shelf.

Now the next part is key: scan the nearby titles on the surrounding shelves. What do you see? Grab any other titles that may be of interest to you. If you find anything interesting, repeat the steps above. Check the Table of Contents and Chapter headings as usual. If there is nothing relevant, then move on. Repeat this process until you think you have what you need or cannot carry any more.

Of Truth

Francis Bacon Edited by John Pfannkuchen

WHAT is truth? said jesting Pilate, and would not stay for an answer. Certainly there be that delight in giddiness, and count it an obligation to believe in something; affecting free will in thinking, as well as in acting. And though those philosophers are gone, there are still certain discoursing wits of the same veins, though there's not as much blood in them as was in those of the ancients.

But it is not only the difficulty and labor which men take in finding out the truth, nor again that when it is found it imposes upon men's thoughts, that favors lying; but a natural though corrupt love of the lie itself.

One of the later Greek schools examines the matter and concludes that men love lying, whether they do it for pleasure, as with poets, or for profit, as with the merchant; they lie for the lie's sake. But I cannot tell; the answer is a naked and open daylight that does not show the masks and mummeries and triumphs of the world half so stately and daintily as candlelight. Truth may be the price of a pearl that looks best during the day, but it's not worth the price of a diamond that looks best in any light. A mixture of a lie always adds pleasure. Does anyone doubt that if vain opinions, flattering hopes, false valuations, imaginations, and the like were taken out of men's minds, that it would leave their minds poor shrunken things, full of melancholy and indisposition, and unpleasing to themselves?

One of the fathers, in great severity, called poetry vinum dæmonum [devils' wine], because it fills the imagination, and yet it contains the shadow of a lie. But it is not the lie that passes through the mind that does damage, but the lie that sinks in and settles. But regardless of how these things are in men's depraved judgments and affections, truth, which only judges itself, teaches that the search for truth (the flirting or wooing of it), the knowledge of truth (the presence of it), and the belief of truth (which is the enjoying of it), is the sovereign good of human nature. No other creature can know the truth like humankind.

The first creature of God, in the works of the days, was the light of the sense; the last was the light of reason; and ever since his work on the Sabbath has illuminated his Spirit. First God breathes light upon the face of chaos; then he breathes light into the face of man; and still he breathes and inspires light into the face of his chosen.

A poet once said that it is a pleasure to stand upon the shore and to see ships tossed upon the sea; a pleasure to stand in the window of a castle and to see a battle and the adventures thereof below: but no pleasure is comparable to the standing upon the vantage ground of truth (a hill not to be commanded, and where the air is always clear and serene), and to see the errors and wanderings and mists and tempests in the vale below; so long as this prospect always be with pity, and not with swelling or pride.

Certainly it is heaven upon earth to have a man's mind move in charity, rest in providence, and turn upon the poles of truth. To pass from theological and philosophical truth to the truth of civil business; it would be admitted even by those who don't practice it that clear and round dealing is the honor of man's nature, and that mixture of falsehood is like alloy in coin of gold and silver, which may make the metal stronger and lighter, but corrupts it. For these winding and crooked courses are the goings of the serpent; which moves basely upon the belly, and not upon the feet. There is no vice that covers a man with so much shame as to be found false and untrustworthy.

And therefore Montaigne said prettily, when he asked why lying should be such a disgrace and such an odious accusation. He said, If it were well considered, to say that a man lies, is to say that he is brave towards God and a coward towards men. Because a lie faces God, and shrinks from man. Surely the wickedness of falsehood and breach of faith cannot possibly be so highly expressed, as in that it shall be the last peal to call the judgments of God upon the generations of men;

it being foretold that when Christ comes, he shall not find faith upon the earth.

References, Sources, Citations, and Quotations

John Pfannkuchen

Every year that I teach the same basic essay, there always seems to be some confusion of terminology, between the words, "source, reference, text," and "quote".

I must admit that for the longest time the exact borders between these words has eluded me as well. But I now know, conventionally, a reference is a "connection" in writing to a source. This connection is what's called reference, and a source is a text that one references, that the essayist mentions in their essay. When one references a text it becomes a source for our essay.

The problem is that people will often confuse sources with references—which is a bit like confusing a telephone wire with the person you're calling. For example if your instructor says "your essay requires 3 references," you should ask whether they mean 3 references to 3 sources or if you should make 3 references to a single source. Because technically the reference is just a connection to the source. What they should say is "reference three outside sources," or something to that effect.

Here's another point of endless confusion. People often conflate the words reference and citation. But a citation is when the essayist tells the reader exactly where the source being referenced came from, where and when it was published, and who wrote it. Usually this is done with MLA or APA "parenthetical citation" (Like This) that points to an endnote or works cited page, where more information on the source can be got.

As for the difference between "reference" and "quotation" I will say that there are two kinds of references: paraphrases and quotations. They are both references, and they both must be cited in modern college courses. Many new students have the mistaken believe that if they "put something into their own words" that do not need to cite it. But that's wrong! How many times have I heard that, and just shaken my head? In modern academics students are expected to cite all of their references—whether they be paraphrased (put into their own words) or quoted directly from a source! The point is to always share with the reader where they can find the exact source being referenced! It doesn't matter how it's referenced.

Now, here's another matter that weighs on me in the middle of the night: whether or not to quote directly, or to paraphrase, a given source. Have you ever been sitting there, looking at an essay, trying to make a reference to another text, and wonder to yourself: should I quote this or paraphrase it? I have. But I can tell you that I have come across the answer and I think it's quite common sense.

For me it all boils down to what I'm writing about. I quote when I'm writing about the words themselves (not just their meaning), and I paraphrase when I'm writing about the meaning behind the words (and altering them is easier for the reader than quoting). I choose what to quote the same way that I choose what to paraphrase. I paraphrase if I don't plan on commenting on the way the source is phrased. This way my reference will lose nothing by being put it into my own words. And conversely, I only quote if I plan to comment on the way a source is phrased. I ask myself what exactly the actual phrasing is adding to my essay before including it. If at all possible, I default to paraphrasing.

I try to avoid the appearance of having created a patchwork of other's ideas and having branded the result as my own.

When writing fiction I paraphrase a character's dialog in the third person like so: John rambled on and on endlessly about the coming of the robot-Dinosaur Apocalypse.

Direct dialog in fiction: John cried, "They're coming for us with their long robot necks and their big swishy tails!"

A direct quote in an essay is the same as direct dialog in fiction, except I use the surname instead of the given name, and I use a citation: Pfannkuchen writes, "They're coming for us with their long robot necks and their big swishy tails" (1).

Notice how the end of sentence punctuation falls outside of the sentence when using a (parenthetical) citation? That is standard parenthetical citation style--in particular MLA. Another popular style, called APA would look something like this: Pfannkuchen writes, "They're coming for us with their long robot necks and their big swishy tails" (Pfannkuchen, 2018).

Also notice how, in all the above examples, it is clear who is speaking, or whose ideas are being expressed? In essay writing I always introduce the work of others to make it clear whose ideas are whose. It should never be vague or difficult to tell if a certain line or idea is either mine, author A's or author B's. The easiest way to affect this clarity is with plain English: "Author writes, 'Quote...'." I prefer the "writes" verb because it is plain and simple, and doesn't distract from the content being discussed.

In most cases the first time I quote or paraphrase from a source I try to include some context or background about that source so that my reader understands it's place in the development of my ideas.

Murder as a Fine Art

Thomas De Quincy Edited by John Pfannkuchen

A new paper on Murder as a Fine Art might open thus: that on the model of those Gentlemen Radicals who had voted a monument to Palmer, etc., it was proposed to erect statues to such murderers as should by their next-of-kin, or other person interested in their glory, make out a claim either of superior atrocity, or, in equal atrocity, of superior neatness, continuity of execution, perfect preparation or felicitous originality, smoothness or curiosa felicitas (elaborate felicity). The men who murdered the cat, as we read in the Newgate Calendar, were good, but Williams better who murdered the baby. And perhaps (but the hellish felicity of the last act makes us demur) Fielding was superior. For you never hear of a fire swallowing up a fire, or a rain stopping a deluge (for this would be a reign of Kilkenny cats); but what fire, deluge, or Kilkenny cats could not do, Fielding proposed, viz., to murder the murderers, to become himself the Nemesis. Fielding was the murderer of murderers in a double sense—rhetorical and literal. But that was, after all, a small matter compared with the fine art of the man calling himself Outis, on which for a moment we must dwell. Outis—so at all events he was called, but doubtless he indulged in many aliases—at Nottingham joined vehemently and sincerely, as it seemed, in pursuit of a wretch taxed with having murdered, twelve years previously, a wife and two children at Halifax, which wretch (when all the depositions were before the magistrate) turned out to be the aforesaid Mr. Outis. That suggests a wide field of speculation and reference.

Note the power of murderers as fine-art professors to make a new start, to turn the corner, to retreat upon the road they have come, as though it were new to them, and to make diversions that disarm suspicion. This they owe to fortunate obscurity, which attests anew the wonderful compensations of life; for celebrity and power combine to produce drawbacks.

A foreigner who lands in Calcutta at an hour which nobody can name, and endeavors to effect a sneaking entrance at the postern-gate of the governor-general's palace, may be a decent man; but this we know, that he has cut the towing-rope which bound his own boat to the great ark of his country. It may be that, in leaving Paris or Naples, he was simply cutting the connection with creditors who showed signs of attachment not good for his health. But it may also be that he ran away by the blaze of a burning inn, which he had fired in order to hide three throats which he had cut, and nine purses which he had stolen. There is no guarantee for such a man's character. Have we, then, no such rascals at home? No, not in the classes standing favorably for promotion. The privilege of safe criminality, not liable to exposure, is limited to classes crowded together like leaves in Vallombrosa; for them to run away into some mighty city, Manchester or Glasgow, is to commence life anew. They turn over a new leaf with a vengeance. Many are the carpenters, bricklayers, bakers' apprentices, etc., who are now living decently in Bristol, Newcastle, Hull, Liverpool, after marrying sixteen wives, and leaving families to the care of twelve separate parishes. That scamp is at this moment circulating and gyrating in society, like a respectable totem, though we don't know his exact name, who, if he were pleased to reveal himself in seventeen parts of this kingdom, where (to use the police language) he has been 'wanted' for some years, would be hanged seventeen times running, besides putting seventeen Government rewards into the pockets of seventeen policemen. Oh, reader, you little know the unutterable romances perpetrated for ever in our most populous empire, under cloud of night and distance and utter poverty, Mark that—of utter poverty. Wealth is power; but it is a jest in comparison of poverty. Splendor is power; but it is a joke to obscurity. To be poor, to be obscure, to be a baker's apprentice or a tailor's journeyman, throws a power about a man, clothes him with attributes of ubiquity, really with those privileges of concealment which in the ring of Gyges were but fabulous. Is it a king, is it a sultan, that such a man rivals? Oh, friend, he rivals a spiritual power.

Two men are on record, perhaps many more might have been on that record, who wrote so many books, and perpetrated so many pamphlets, that at fifty they had forgotten much of their own literary villainies, and at sixty they commenced with murderous ferocity a series of answers to arguments which it was proved upon them afterwards that they themselves had emitted at thirty—thus coming round with volleys of small shot on their own heads, as the Whispering Gallery at St. Paul's begins to retaliate any secrets you have committed to its keeping in echoing thunders after a time, or as Sir John Mandeville under Arctic skies heard in May all those curses thawing, and exploding like minute-guns, which had been frozen up in November. Even like those self-replying authors, even like those self-reverberators in St. Paul's, even like those Arctic practitioners in cursing, who drew bills and post obits in malediction, which were to be honored after the death of winter, many men are living at this moment in merry England who have figured in so many characters, illustrated so many villages, run away from so many towns, and performed the central part in so many careers, that were the character, the village, the town, the career, brought back with all its circumstances to their memories, positively they would fail to recognize their own presence or incarnation in their own acts and bodies.

We have all read the story told by Addison of a sultan, who was persuaded by a dervish to dip his head into a basin of enchanted water, and thereupon found himself upon some other globe, a son in a poor man's family, married after certain years the woman of his heart, had a family of seven children whom he painfully brought up, went afterwards through many persecutions, walked pensively by the seashore meditating some escape from his miseries, bathed in the sea as a relief from the noon-day heat, and on lifting up his head from the waves found himself lifting up his head from the basin into which that cursed dervish had persuaded him to dip. And when he would have cudgeled the holy man for that long life of misery which had, through his means, been inflicted upon himself, behold! the holy man proved by affidavit that, in this world, at any rate (where only he could be punishable), the life had lasted but thirty-three seconds. Even so do the dark careers of many amongst our obscure and migratory villains from years shrink up to momentary specks, or, by their very multitude, altogether evanesce. Burke and Hare, it is well known, had lost all count of their several murders; they no more remembered, or could attempt to remember, their separate victims, than a respectable old banker of seventy-three can remember all the bills with their endorsements made payable for half-a-century at his bank; or than Foote's turnpike-keeper, who had kept all the toll-bar tickets to Kensington for forty-eight years, pretended to recollect the features of all the men who had delivered them at his gate. For a time, perhaps, Burke (who was a man of fine sensibility) had a representative vision of spasms, and struggles, and convulsions, terminating in a ten-pound note endorsed by Dr. Someone. Hare, on the other hand, was a man of principle, a man that you could depend upon—order a corpse for Friday, and on Friday you had it—but he had no feeling whatsoever. Yet see the unity of result for him and Burke. For both alike all troublesome recollections gathered into one blue haze of heavenly abstractions: orders executed with fidelity, checks on the bankers to be crossed and passed and cashed, are no more remembered. That is the acme of perfection in our art.

One great class of criminals I am aware of in past times as having specially tormented myself—the class who have left secrets, riddles, behind them. What business has any man to bequeath a conundrum to all posterity, unless he leaves in some separate channel the solution? This must have been done in malice, and for the purpose of annoying us, lest we should have too much proper enjoyment of life when he should have gone. For nobody knows whether the scoundrel could have solved it himself—too like in that respect to some charades which, in my boyish days (but then I had the excuse of youth, which they had not), I not infrequently propounded to young ladies. Take this as a specimen: My first raises a little hope; my second very little indeed; and my whole is a vast roar of despair. No young lady could ever solve it; neither could I. We all had to give it up. A charade that only needs an answer, which, perhaps, some distant generation may supply, is but a half and half, tentative approach to this. Very much of this nature was the genius or Daimon (don't say Demon) of Socrates. How many thousands of learned writers and printers have gone to sleep over too profound attempts to solve that, which Socrates ought to have been able to solve at sight. I am myself of opinion that it was a dram-bottle, which someone raised a ghost to explain.

Then the Entelecheia of Aristotle; did you ever read about that, excellent reader? Most people fancy it to have meant some unutterable crotchet in metaphysics, some horrible idea (lest the police should be after it) without a name; that is, until the Stagyrite repaired the injustice of his conduct by giving it a pretty long one. My opinion now, as you are anxious to know it, is, that it was a lady, a sweetheart of Aristotle's; for what was to hinder Aristotle having a sweetheart?

I dare say Thomas Aquinas, dry and arid as he was, raised his unprincipled eyes to some Neapolitan beauty, began a sonnet to some lady's eyebrow, though he might forget to finish it. And my belief is that this lady, ambitious as Semele, wished to be introduced as an eternal jewel into the great vault of her lover's immortal Philosophy, which was to travel much farther and agitate far longer than his royal pupil's conquests. Upon that Aristotle, keeping her hand, said: 'My love, I'll think of it.' And then it occurred to him, that in the very heavens many lovely ladies, Andromeda, Cassiopeia, Ariadne, etc., had been placed as constellations in that map which many chronologists suppose to have been prepared for the use of the ship Argo, a whole generation before the Trojan war. Berenice, though he could not be aware of that, had interest even to procure a place in that map for her ringlets; and of course for herself she might have. Considering which, Aristotle said: 'Hang me! if I don't put her among the ten Categories!' On after thoughts he put her higher, for an Entelecheia is as much above a Category as our Padishah Victoria is above a Turkish sultan. 'But now, Stag,' said the lady (privileged as a sweetheart she called him Stag, though everybody else was obliged to call him Stagyrite), 'how will they know it's meant for me, Stag?' Upon which I am sorry to say the philosopher fell to cursing and swearing, bestowing blessings on his own optics and on posterity's, meaning yours and mine, saying: 'Let them find it out.' Well, now, you see I have found it out. But that is more than I hope for my crypto-criminals, and therefore I take this my only way of giving them celebration and malediction in one breath.

FOOTNOTES

Notwithstanding what he had written in the essay on the 'Essenes,' no doubt De Quincey, if he had completed this paper, could not have escaped characteristic, and perhaps grimly humorous, references of his own to the Sicarii, of whom Josephus has a good deal to tell in his 'Jewish War'; for it seems to us his thoughts were bearing directly that way. Josephus says of the Sicarii: 'In these days there arose another sort of robbers in Jerusalem, who were named Sicarii, who slew men in the day-time and in the middle of the city, more especially at the festivals. There they mixed with the multitude, and having concealed little daggers under their garments, with these they stabbed those that were their enemies; and when any fell down dead, the murderers joined the bystanders in expressing their indignation; so that from their plausibilities they could by no means be discovered. The first man that was slain by them was Jonathan the high-priest, after which many were slain every day.'—Ed.

'Postern-gate.' See the legend of Sir Eustace the Crusader, and the good Sir Hubert, who 'sounded the horn which he alone could sound,' as told by Wordsworth.

Made in the USA
Middletown, DE
02 February 2019